# LOSING FAITH

# LOSING FAITH

## HOW THE GROVE SURVIVORS LED THE DECLINE OF INTEL'S CORPORATE CULTURE

BOB COLEMAN

LOGAN SHRINE

ISBN 10: 0-9791681-0-4
ISBN 13: 978-0-9791681-0-9
Library of Congress Control Number: 2006910460

FIRST EDITION

Printed in the United States of America

Book's website: www.losing-faith.com


10  9  8  7  6  5  4  3  2  1

# CONTENTS

# Acknowledgments

The authors would like to acknowledge those current and former Intel employees who endeavor to continue the heritage of company greatness. We would also like to acknowledge the following authors, whose experience, insights, and research helped to substantiate our observations: Tim Jackson, Jack Welch, Lou Gerstner, Jim Collins, Larry Bossidy, Dr. Jeffrey Pfeffer, Dr. Geary Rummler, Alan Brache, Dr. Lawrence Peter, and Dr. Clayton Christensen.

# Preface

The authors would like to state up front that we have been Intel employees in good standing, with respectable (at times outstanding) performance reviews. We wrote this book not because we became disgruntled, but rather because we became intolerant of a once-productive culture that has deteriorated and impeded company performance. We felt that the best way to begin changing this culture was to write this book and bring external scrutiny to bear on the company, as most internal efforts to effect change have been unsuccessful.

# PROLOGUE

# Fireworks at the Shareholder Meeting

> We all know that in the absence of strong corporate cultures, companies turn bureaucratic.[1]
>
> Andy Grove

> We need to continually assess and challenge the vitality of our culture. And it is not just the job of management. Every employee should feel that responsibility.[2]
>
> Craig Barrett

At the Intel Corp. 2006 shareholder meeting, management received some harsh questions from shareholders about the semiconductor maker's sagging stock price over the last five years

One long-time shareholder went so far as to suggest that Intel take a page from Hewlett-Packard, whose results and stock price have improved dramatically since it brought in Mark Hurd to replace Carly Fiorina as CEO.

"I suggest that someone ought to be fired in Intel," the stockholder said during the meeting. "My question is who?"

Craig Barrett, Intel's chairman, visibly uncomfortable with the question, conceded that the company's recent financial results and stock price have been "unsatisfactory." But he defensively retorted that a more reasonable form of "punishment" for management would come in a reduction in bonuses and stock-based compensation for 2006.

At the previous year's annual shareholders' meeting, questions like this had been noticeably absent. Why? What was different in 2005? Was

---

[1] http://www.gsb.stanford.edu/news/headlines/2004arbuckleaward.shtml.
[2] Intel employee website.

it the stock price? After rising from a low of roughly $22 at the beginning of the year, the stock had met resistance around $25 but had peaked after the shareholders' meeting, only to finish around $25 again at the end of the year. However, a look at the stock's performance from 2003 to May 2006 shows that the stock has been trading relatively sideways throughout this three-year period, with investors taking advantage of one- to three-dollar movements in either direction. The problem really couldn't have been the stock price, so why weren't shareholders "confrontational" in 2005?

To people who attended both shareholder meetings, the obvious answer was the presence at the 2005 meeting of Chairman Andy Grove, whom shareholders nostalgically revered for his connection with past stock performance, even as they conveniently neglected to confront current management (Barrett) about the stock's recent performance. Now that Andy Grove is far removed from the Intel spotlight, shareholders' sentiments are different, as a subtle change in the handling of questions at the shareholder meetings seems to indicate. Andy's admirable command of the 2005 shareholder meeting was clear from the way he deferred questions not specifically directed to him to Craig Barrett and Paul Otellini for answering. By contrast, when the question about firing someone was asked in 2006, it was not directed to any specific person on the Intel panel, yet Craig Barrett took responsibility for answering it. To an outsider, this would appear normal; to an Intel insider, however, this was an "inflection point" or change that ironically incriminated Barrett and his performance as Chief Executive Officer (CEO).

Now that Andy Grove was gone, shareholders were not reluctant to confront Intel management. There had obviously been pent-up frustration with the stock's performance over the past five years, and that frustration could be released now that the revered and feared persona of Andy Grove was no longer "steering the ship" at the annual shareholder meeting.

This inflection point, as borne out by the tenor of the questions at shareholder meetings, is merely a microcosm of the larger change that occurred within the Intel culture when leadership passed from Andy Grove to Craig Barrett. The strong performance of Intel stock during the Grove years could be directly correlated to the effectiveness of Intel's culture during that time. This correlation also holds true during the succeeding era under Craig Barrett, but it points in the opposite direction.

What is the first thing that comes to mind when you hear the term *corporate culture*? Is it a company's mission statement? A list of the corporate values? Or is it the names of prominent business leaders who have shaped their respective companies by their actions? Although the question of what influences corporate culture the most—its mission statement, its company values, or its leaders—largely depends upon the individual company. For the most part, people agree that leaders and leadership actions are the most important.

There can be no doubt that in the case of Intel Corporation, the names of Robert Noyce, Gordon Moore, and Andy Grove come to mind when the question of culture arises. The actions and behaviors of these three legends—especially Andy Grove—and employee responses to those actions and behaviors are what shaped the culture of Intel, much more than did any of Intel's annual mission statements or even its venerated Values.

For the purposes of this book, it's extremely important to distinguish between leadership actions and the company's published Values in order to understand the relative importance of each to the cultural health of Intel. This distinction is vital, since Intel's more recent CEOs, Craig Barrett and Paul Otellini, have frequently invoked and encouraged adherence to the Intel Values as the primary means of strengthening the culture and improving company performance. In the eyes of rank-and-file employees, however, very little effort has been made to hold middle and senior managers accountable for their own behaviors when these have been inappropriate and at variance with the published Values.

The Intel Values, it should be noted, were not published until eighteen years *after* the founding of the company. Interesting, too, is the fact that none of Intel's founders penned the Intel Values; rather, this act was delegated to Bob Reed, who served as Intel's senior vice president of finance and administration in the mid 1980s. Did the fact that Reed held a position of great responsibility make him the person most qualified to lay out the corporate values for a company he didn't found? Probably not. In fact, Reed himself pointed out that Intel "already had a very well-developed culture" before the Values were published.[3] These interesting facts suggest that to understand the culture of Intel, we must look beyond

---

[3] Intel employee website.

the words of the published Values and pay close attention to the behaviors and actions of its leaders, and to the responses of employees to those behaviors and actions.

That being said, is there anything wrong with the content of the Intel Values? Not at all. But because actions speak louder than words, the Values should not be taken at face value as the primary measure of Intel's cultural health. Andy Grove himself provides a case in point: he was a great proponent of the Intel Values once they were published, and he tried to get the company to live by them, yet he could not undo what his examples had created in the culture in the eighteen years preceding the publication of those of Values. One reason for this is that, as Jim Collins and Jerry Porras point out, "the extent to which a company attains consistent alignment with the ideology [values] counts more than the content of the ideology."[4] In essence, as we will show, the Intel Values were DOA (dead on arrival) because they were not consistent with the established leadership and employee behaviors that preceded them.

It could be argued that when Bob Reed wrote the Intel Values in 1986, they accurately captured the egalitarian ideals of Robert Noyce and Gordon Moore and that they also reflected the past actions of the few employees who built Intel's core competencies, fab (manufacturing) process technology and microprocessor design. Maybe this was the case, but the Values did not accurately reflect Intel's culture at the time, because most employees had already become reactive and were cowering under the confrontational, in-your-face management style of Andy Grove, which trickled down throughout the entire organization.

After the publication of the Intel Values came the boom years of the 1990s, when the company was growing and many employees were making money through their stock options. During that period, no one had time to think about the softer side of the culture because everyone was too busy helping Intel keep up with the demand for microprocessors. People would only look up to smell the money and then put their heads back down, their noses to the grindstone. As a result, a culture of greed set in, and in the company where "you own[ed] your career,"[5] employees

---

[4] James C. Collins and Jerry I. Porras, *Built to Last* (New York, NY: HarperCollins, 1994), 69.
[5] Andy Grove, *Only the Paranoid Survive* (New York, NY: Doubleday, 1996), 6.

became skilled at self-promotion, competing against each other, and managing upward—in essence, "gaming" the system—for personal gain. Furthermore, an unspoken rite of passage was established whereby employees who had survived the extremities of the Grove-led "grindstone" era now advanced in the environment of cut-throat competition and became the new middle and senior managers as the company's headcount grew dramatically under Craig Barrett's leadership in the mid to late 1990s.

When the Internet bubble burst in 2000, the company's performance became more of a concern, and many Intel employees voiced the opinion that the corporate culture was not "what it used to be." Well, what had it been before? As mentioned above, when employees were getting rich from stock option appreciation, the thought of culture was far from their minds: rather, their thoughts were focused on what they were going to spend their money on when they retired as high-tech millionaires. The "Grove Survivors"[6] were quick to point the finger at new hires as the source of Intel's cultural woes—"They don't understand the way things work at Intel." On the flip side, newer employees became indignant with how Grove Survivors were not held accountable for their repeated failures, which were caused in large part by behaviors that were inconsistent with the published Intel Values.

In the midst of recent employee unrest over the culture, Intel's senior management seems to be in denial. The year 2004 was filled with company-wide discussions over the strength of the Intel culture, and since that time Intel's senior leaders have maintained that the corporate culture is vibrant, strong, and unchanged from the glory days of the personal computer boom years. Despite these claims, there can be no denying that the boom days are over, as rival semiconductor company AMD (Advanced Micro Devices) is taking a larger share of the market segment in central processing units (CPUs)[7], and Intel employees have become sober regarding their stock options.

The fact is many senior managers are lost and not sure how to get back

---

[6] Employees who survived the extremely demanding, fear-driven culture under the leadership of Andy Grove and have become entitled to certain privileges under subsequent CEOs. As we explain throughout the book, a familial bond exists among Grove Survivors because they've shared the extreme highs and lows of life at Intel.

[7] In 2006 there have been scores of articles about AMD's market share gains in server, desktop, and notebook market segments.

to those glory days of ever-increasing stock appreciation. In the boom years, many of them were too busy to see the forest through the trees, and now that they have the time, they seem uncertain about what to do. Andy Grove was a tough disciplinarian who wouldn't hesitate to humiliate managers if he saw fit to, and these same managers—who, out of fear, learned not to take risks and challenge the status quo during the Grove years—are running Intel today. Perhaps many of them appear to be spineless and unable to lead because of how they were treated, but in any case, they now give lip service to the Intel Values without living up to them.

This book acknowledges that there are differing views on the Intel culture: (1) Grove Survivor senior managers deny there is a problem with it; (2) Grove Survivors who acknowledge that there is a problem (mostly middle managers and senior-level individual contributors) contend that it stems from the numerous new hires that came to Intel and diluted the culture during the late 1990s and early 2000s; and (3) newer hires believe that Intel's senior and middle managers—mostly Grove Survivors—have not set a good example and are not being held accountable for repeated failures that stem from violations of the Intel Values.

Which of these views is the most accurate? The experience and observations of the authors clearly point to the last view, that the Grove Survivors have dominated Intel's culture and are primarily responsible for its decline and the resultant decline in company performance. This cultural domination is manifest in a situation that might be disputed by Intel Lifers[8] and Grove Survivors, but that will be revealed in this book: not all people are treated equally at Intel. Grove Survivors have created a mammoth bureaucracy whose elite members are entitled to repeated failures without consequences, and decision authority without accountability: in short, they enjoy the benefits of a familial bond that protects the family member's position and employment in all but the most extreme of circumstances.

This book will attempt to identify and explain the key cultural inflection points that made the Intel culture what it is today. It will compare actual employee behaviors with the published Intel Values and draw conclusions about whether prevalent behaviors within Intel's culture will ultimately help or hurt the company's prospects for growth

---

[8] Employees whose entire working careers have been at Intel.

and sustained operational performance.

From the authors' vantage point, it has become exceedingly clear that traditional means (such as "open door" policies and elevating to managers) for addressing the problem of the Intel culture—and hence, its performance—are not working. We believe the culture has changed for the worse and that it is necessary to force public scrutiny on specific aspects of the culture in order to trigger acknowledgement of these cultural problems and lift the veil of senior management denial that continues to impede the company's performance. It is our primary hope that this book—a direct appeal to the Intel community of shareholders, employees, and customers—will be a catalyst to bring about necessary changes from within and from outside the company, to truly cleanse and reinvigorate Intel's culture, and to open the way for a new era of innovation and growth.

Additionally, we hope that an acknowledgement of the destructive behaviors identified in this book will be of value to anyone who is a part of or interacts with large and powerful organizations, where the need for change seems obvious to the objective eye, yet next-to-impossible to achieve without the right leadership.

Finally, we realistically recognize that it is very unlikely that this book will be a catalyst for change within a powerful organization such as Intel. Therefore, if for nothing else, we hope you get some entertainment value from reading this modest work on the paradoxical and anomalous culture of Intel Corporation.

## The Intel Values

We have included below a table with the published Intel Values so that the reader may review and understand what those values are, and thus (within the context of this book's analysis) take into consideration how observed actual behaviors are inconsistent with the published Values.[9]

---

[9] www.intel.com/jobs/workplace/values.htm

## Published Intel Values

| Risk Taking | Discipline |
|---|---|
| • Foster innovation and creative thinking<br>• Embrace change and challenge the status quo<br>• Listen to all ideas and viewpoints<br>• Learn from our successes and mistakes<br>• Encourage and reward informed risk taking | • Conduct business with uncompromising integrity and professionalism<br>• Ensure a safe, clean and injury-free workplace<br>• Make and meet commitments<br>• Properly plan, fund and staff projects<br>• Pay attention to detail |
| **Quality** | **Results Orientation** |
| • Achieve the highest standards of excellence<br>• Do the right things right<br>• Continuously learn, develop and improve<br>• Take pride in our work | • Set challenging and competitive goals<br>• Focus on output<br>• Assume responsibility<br>• Constructively confront and solve problems<br>**Execute flawlessly** |
| **Great Place To Work** | **Customer Orientation** |
| • Be open and direct<br>• Promote a challenging work environment that develops our diverse workforce<br>• Work as a team with respect and trust for each other<br>• Win and have fun<br>• Recognize and reward accomplishments<br>• Manage performance fairly and firmly<br>• Be an asset to our communities worldwide | • Listen and respond to our customers, suppliers and stakeholders<br>• Clearly communicate mutual intentions and expectations<br>• Deliver innovative and competitive products and services<br>• Make it easy to work with us<br>• Be vendor of choice |

# LEADERSHIP

# Chapter 1

# Leadership Actions that Shaped the Culture

Preach always, and if necessary use words.[10]

St. Francis of Assisi

The number one failure of leaders is their failure to reproduce other leaders.[11]

Dr. Jack Elwood

Who would ever have thought that the profundity of St. Francis of Assisi would be applicable to a high-tech behemoth like Intel? The 21st-century's corollary to the 13th-century mystic's adage is that actions speak louder than words. Even Teddy Roosevelt said, "Speak softly and carry a big stick." As eloquent as Roosevelt was with words, it was his actions that shaped the political landscape of the country. Great leaders *demonstrate* what they want others to do and they serve as role models. Often, however, leaders remain unaware of how their actions are interpreted unless they seek feedback or are inclined to self-reflection, which can be expressed in different ways—many great leaders have written autobiographies, management books, or reflective observations about their reign, for instance.

If you examine the DNA of leaders in great companies like GE and IBM, you find that these extraordinary leaders possess a rare combination of determination, ability to take risks, and humility. Such individuals reach the pinnacle of leadership performance perhaps because of this uncommon combination of characteristics, which enables them to foster in their organizations the innovation and discipline

---

[10] www.franciscan.org.au/companions.html.

[11] Quote of the day, www.excite.com.

necessary for growth and high operational performance.

When people think of "Intel" and "leadership," one name comes to mind: Andy Grove. This inextricable connection is not only prevalent in the public mind, but is also indelibly etched in Andy Grove's mind, such that he refers to Intel as his "family,"[12] a fact which, in many respects, positions him as the "father" by virtue of his leadership throughout the history of the company. And while there hasn't been a transfer of *physical* DNA from Andy to the company, there can be no doubt that his *behavioral* DNA has been passed on to the corporate culture of Intel.

The general public, when thinking of Intel's leadership, may tend to overlook the role that Intel's two original founders, Robert Noyce and Gordon Moore, played in the development of Intel's culture. This oversight is easy to understand, given the towering persona of Andy Grove. However, it is only by understanding some of the founding principles of Intel and the personalities of Noyce and Moore that a more complete and meaningful assessment of Andy Grove and Intel's culture can be appreciated. It stands to reason also that Intel would have its share of great leaders at all levels of the organization, given the strength of its early CEOs. However, we will attempt to show the flaws in this assumption by shedding new light on how the behaviors of Intel's prominent leaders have given birth to and shaped Intel's corporate culture.

## The Era of Innovation

It doesn't take a thorough investigation and analysis of the founding of Intel to understand how much of its success is owed to the remarkable power and influence of its two founders, Robert Noyce and Gordon Moore. Given their history of success in starting Fairchild Semiconductor in 1957, which put "Silicon Valley" on the map, it was relatively simple for them to raise $2.5 million (in one afternoon) to start the new venture that would become Intel. The reputations of Noyce and Moore, General Manager and Director, respectively, of research and development at Fairchild Semiconductor, spoke volumes more than any detailed business plan could have.

From the earliest days, Noyce and Moore were exceptionally keen on attracting and selecting talent and putting talented people in the right

---

[12] 2005 Intel Sales and Marketing Conference.

positions. Wanting to avoid the problems that had plagued Fairchild, Noyce and Moore set out to make Intel "a partnership of equals so that [employees] could discuss any of the problems that arose."[13] Noyce, in particular, had been frustrated with his lack of control over the business at Fairchild, so he wanted to make sure Intel's culture exemplified an egalitarian spirit where day-to-day decisions and operations were more democratic than autocratic in nature. To further cement their egalitarian intentions, Noyce and Moore decided to give employees an equity position in the company in the form of stock options, an emerging practice within Silicon Valley at the time.

On the surface, the personalities of the two founders seemed quite different. Noyce was gregarious, athletic, and handsome—the life of the party—yet he displayed a Midwestern charm and sensibility. Moore, on the other hand, was soft-spoken and extremely modest, a model of equanimity.[14] Despite these apparent differences, the qualities of both men were highly complementary, with Noyce as the charismatic entrepreneur and Moore as the visionary technologist of the company. Both Noyce and Moore were modest, as manifest by their being excellent listeners who displayed a sincere interest in the ideas and concerns of others. They treated people well. As Peter Seligmann, executive director of Conservation International recalls of his first meeting with Moore, "I was struck by his gentleness and his humility and deep interest in everything."[15] Furthermore, both Noyce and Moore had an impressive history of success at overcoming significant obstacles, which speaks volumes to their determination. Noyce, for example, didn't become the co-inventor of the integrated circuit without having the tenacity to persevere through countless setbacks along the path to this world-changing invention. Another similarity between the founders can be seen in the way they channeled their ambition into making Intel a great company, much more than seeking their own personal gain. And as a final measure of their greatness, history shows that both of these men established an organization whose stature increased after their departures.

---

[13] How We Got Started, Gordon Moore, September 2003, Fortune – Small Business, www.fortune.com/fortune/smallbusiness/articles/0,15114,475592-1,00.html
[14] Tim Jackson, *Inside Intel* (New York, NY: Penguin Group, 1997), 19.
[15] Gordon Moore, Heather Clancy, November 8, 2000, www.crn.com.

Noyce was endowed with powerful charisma that he used to great advantage to *inspire* others to new heights of performance "for the good of Intel," not "for the good of Bob Noyce" or to *drive* others to perform out of fear. This is an important distinction, because it shows that Intel was not primarily a showcase for his unique skills, as it was, in many respects, for Andy Grove. Rather, by unselfishly channeling his charismatic gifts toward the good of Intel, the semiconductor industry, and American manufacturing, Noyce became a peerless statesman of the industry he helped establish. He well and truly deserved his moniker, "The Father of Silicon Valley."

Moore, by nature much more reserved than either Noyce or Grove, proved to be the perfect foil for the more notable leaders of Intel. A close look at Moore presents the fascinating case of an individual who was modest, yet brilliant. He showed an uncanny ability to cut to the heart of complexities and, more importantly, to identify significant strategic factors in the realms of technology, business, and management of people. Three brief examples illustrate this. First, he formulated the principle that became famous as "Moore's Law," which accurately predicted, back in 1965 when scant data were available, the growth rate of semiconductor complexity and power over time. A second and lesser-known detail that illustrates his business savvy took place in the mid 1980s, at the most pivotal point of Intel's history. In the midst of Intel's losses from its struggles in a brutally competitive dynamic random-access memory (DRAM) market, Andy Grove asked Gordon Moore a fateful question: "If we got kicked out and the board brought in a new CEO, what do you think he would do?" It was Gordon, not Andy, who answered without hesitation, "He would get us out of memories." Grove admits to having been *numbed* by this answer and credits Moore, who was chairman and CEO at that time, with providing the encouragement to get Intel started on that difficult yet wildly successful journey out of the DRAM business.[16] Finally, Moore predicted that Intel's mid 1980s directional shift to a focus on microprocessors would require executive staff and other employees to change their areas of knowledge and expertise in order to remain with the company—a prediction that turned out to be dead on. Whether he dealt with technology, business, or people management, Moore had the deep wisdom and piercing insights that

---

[16] Andy Grove, *Only the Paranoid Survive* (New York, NY: Doubleday, 1996), 95.

quietly guided the strategic direction of Intel from its early days into the boom years of the 1990s. Moreover, it's important to note that the actions of Intel's two original founders, Noyce and Moore, were completely consistent with their egalitarian ideals and hopes for the Intel culture. Unfortunately, they failed to document specific company values beyond their noble egalitarian ideals, leaving the Intel culture to be shaped primarily by the mercurial leadership actions of people less noble than themselves.

Notwithstanding the dynamic personalities and impressive track records of Noyce and Moore, it was Andy Grove who would come to dominate the culture of Intel within a few short years of its founding, and the subsequent shaping or morphing of Intel's culture may have gone largely undetected by the two original founders. Grove, being their subordinate, probably wanted to impress them, and no doubt showed them a measure of deference and respect that was not accorded to those who were subordinate to him. It could be further speculated that this situation created an environment where the seeds of "managing upward" were planted in the Intel culture—that is, where managers' upward communications became intentionally rosier than their everyday realities, so they could make themselves look good in the eyes of their superiors. Perhaps this explains why Gordon Moore, when talking of the early days of Intel, reveals such a difference in perspective between himself and Andy Grove.

> The Intel startup was amazingly smooth. We beat our budgets. Our initial idea was that we had five years to get to $25 million in revenue; we actually got to $63 million. We went public in 1971, the first year we had a profit. Because things more or less happened on schedule, I was pretty relaxed about it. If you ask Andy Grove, he says that it was the worst time of his entire life. He was afraid we were going to go bankrupt every week. Either I didn't understand what was going on, or he's more paranoid than I am.[17]

Given the stark contrast between Moore's and Grove's perspectives in this case, it could be expected that their attitudes and behaviors within the workplace would likewise be quite different. In fairness to Andy Grove, this was his first startup, and as the director of operations he must have keenly felt the burden of delivering Intel products, so it stands to

---

[17] How We Got Started, Gordon Moore, September 2003, *Fortune* – Small Business, www.fortune.com/fortune/smallbusiness/articles/0,15114,475592-1,00.html

reason that he would be a bit more "paranoid" than Moore in this situation. And while the results of his high-pressure leadership can't responsibly be disputed, we can certainly call into question some of the unintended long-term consequences that his domineering management style had on the Intel culture.

> In summary, the leadership actions of the two founders, Noyce and Moore, established the foundation for the following Intel Values:
>
> **RISK TAKING**
> ⇒ Foster innovation and creative thinking
> ⇒ Embrace change and challenge the status quo
> ⇒ Listen to all ideas and viewpoints
> ⇒ Learn from our successes and mistakes
> ⇒ Encourage and reward informed risk taking
>
> **CUSTOMER ORIENTATION**
> ⇒ Listen and respond to our customers, suppliers and stakeholders
> ⇒ Clearly communicate mutual intentions and expectations
> ⇒ Deliver innovative and competitive products and services

## The Era of Growth

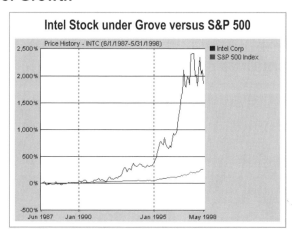

Even people who are only remotely connected to the world of business know that Andy Grove has received universal praise as a "management genius" and "industry visionary." For example, in 1997 he was named Time Magazine's "Man of the Year," and in 2004, *Nightly Business Report* and the Wharton School of Business identified him as the "most influential business person of the last 25 years."[18] Furthermore, the record of Intel's stock-price performance leaves little doubt that he was a dynamic leader who knew how to inspire high levels of performance throughout a large organization. During his tenure as CEO, Intel's stock price beat the market by a factor of roughly ten.[19]

If you reach back into Andy Grove's formative years, it's not a stretch to conclude that he was largely a product of his environment. There can be no doubt that the experiences of his early years—surviving both the Nazis and the communists in Hungary, escaping to the United States, and struggling to get a university education in New York, among other things—helped to develop the fierce tenacity that would not only serve him well in his career at Intel, but be the cornerstone of his legendary leadership. Indeed, Tim Jackson states that Grove "possessed willpower, self-control, and determination in quantities that were given only to one person in a million."[20] Both Noyce and Moore recognized these qualities early on and were willing and even desirous to have Grove take on the tough tasks that they were either reluctant to do or lacked the resolve to do on their own.

On the flip side, however, Grove lacked the modesty of the two original founders, which might help explain the genesis of Intel's legendary reputation for arrogance. Furthermore, notwithstanding his reputation as an industry visionary, Andy Grove is generally given credit for Intel's shift to microprocessors, even though it was Gordon Moore who first said that Intel should get out of memories. That issue aside, our concern lies with his legacy as it pertains to Intel's culture.

One of the key tenets of this book is that Intel's corporate culture changed during the transition from the Noyce-Moore leadership to the Grove leadership: that it clearly went from egalitarianism to authoritarianism. This critical transition has had lasting effects on the behaviors and performance of employees since Grove handed over the CEO reins to Craig Barrett. There can be no doubt that Grove's charismatic, overpowering presence and intimidating confrontational style set the tone for the company's culture—long before the Intel Values (the "inspired standards") were composed and published. Under Grove,

---

[18] www.nightlybusiness.org/Specials/25anniversary/winner.html
[19] moneycentral.msn.com
[20] Tim Jackson, *Inside Intel* (New York, NY: Penguin Group, 1997), 83.

the culture became one where leaders (particularly Grove himself) "inspected" for compliance with their expectations. Managers were expected to understand the details of projects under their stewardships and present data to support their analyses and drive decisions. As a manager under Grove, you would be expected to "do your homework" and have data to support your actions; more importantly, you had to execute your work flawlessly and were held accountable for getting the results to meet your commitments. What truly made Andy Grove a great leader were two necessary qualities: technical competence and the discipline of execution—the ability to implement change and get results.

> **What is meant by technical competence?** It is a combination of theory, skill, and practical knowledge in a specific domain, coupled with the capability and experience to understand the details and distinguish the right from wrong approach or direction in solving a problem in that domain.[21]

What we mean by the discipline of execution is that there were no gaps between a commitment and the actual results. Follow-through was absolutely essential, as was confronting reality and rewarding people who could achieve those results.

Andy "lived" for Intel. He gave his best to Intel and he expected this of everyone. He hired brilliant people; he expected them to execute strategic objectives and plans; and he quickly eliminated those who did not. As we will show further on, however, that winning combination of technical competence and discipline of execution is lacking not only in the subsequent leadership, but is also painfully absent from a wide band of senior and middle managers within the company.

Andy Grove is justifiably proud of his contributions to the creation of a company that has survived generations of technological change and has, in the process, helped put personal computers into the hands of over one billion individuals.[22] He was the primary force driving Intel's phenomenal growth and success. He led one of the world's most powerful technology companies during the digital revolution. No one can take away these indisputable accomplishments, yet a deeper look at his actions as leader of Intel reveals that behavioral "seeds" sown during his

---

[21] The authors developed this definition for the book.
[22] www.nightlybusiness.org/Specials/25anniversary/winner.html

tenure later brought forth unintended "fruits" within the Intel culture—fruits that pre-dated the publishing of the Intel Values and continue to be harvested to this day.

It's well known that Grove had an "in your face" management style and that he did not tolerate poor performance or flawed execution of tasks. Once the Intel Values were published, Andy became a passionate proponent of them (particularly the one invoking "discipline"). He wouldn't hesitate to stop an employee, even if the person were a complete stranger, and ask him or her to recite the Intel Values. By word-of-mouth, employees became motivated to "discipline" themselves and learn the Values so that they would be prepared for such an encounter.

Under Grove's leadership, the company's *actions* demonstrated discipline. This is not to say that the *culture* was a disciplined one, but that employees acted in a disciplined fashion out of fear, primarily, though they may have been motivated also by Andy's charisma and powerful demeanor. By the time the Values were published, employees continued to be motivated by fear, rather than by inherent self-discipline or inspiration by the official company Values. This is an important distinction that had significant cultural effects on Intel after Andy Grove's departure as CEO.

Intel Corporation had been primarily a manufacturer of memory when Andy Grove became its third CEO in 1987. Grove was a technologist by training who later pursued his own interests in management. It was Grove's management fervor that drove Intel to become the world leader in microprocessors, once the decision had been made to get out of DRAMs.

While both Andy Grove and Gordon Moore are universally hailed for their response to the strategic inflection point[23] that forced the company out of the DRAM business, Andy Grove himself admits that he "was asleep when the personal computer came onto the scene [and] for some period of time…did not appreciate the explosive strength that it had as a market for our product…."[24] Perhaps a more humble leader would have

---

[23] "A strategic inflection point is a time in the life of a business when its fundamentals are about to change. That change can mean an opportunity to rise to new heights. But it may just as likely signal the beginning of the end."
http://www.intel.com/pressroom/kits/bios/grove/paranoid.htm.

[24] www.nightlybusiness.org/Specials/25anniversary/winner.html

confronted these market realities more quickly and effectively by changing the company's status quo without first enduring such a painful, protracted beating in the DRAM market. If it can be said that an inflection point *in the culture*—one that directly tied in with the Intel Values ("Learn from our successes and mistakes")—also occurred with the transition from DRAMs to microprocessors, then this provides a starting point from which we can see that demonstrated behaviors did not reflect what would later be published as part of the Intel Values. At this cultural inflection point, the foundation was laid for future behaviors that emerged in the management layers after Andy's transition out of the CEO role.

Throughout the years, there have been many examples of management behaviors failing to mirror published Values. One example stems from the introduction in the mid 1990s of the sub-$1000 personal computer (PC), a market segment that was initially rejected by Intel management (Grove) but quickly targeted by AMD. AMD was willing to adjust its microprocessor technology to meet a customer need and thereby secure the CPU business for this new PC market segment. This move by AMD, with disruptive technology that would alter the course of the PC market by addressing a smaller, less profitable market segment, soon led to the PC's emergence as a dominant market segment worldwide.

The examples of the DRAM market and sub-$1000 PC market indicate that Grove lacked humility, and they help to explain the arrogant, "in-your-face," "we-can-do-anything" culture that emerged under his leadership. Such an attitude has adversely affected the company's desire and ability to listen to customers, perceive market trends, and more importantly, learn from mistakes and then act accordingly. These behaviors, although they seem trivial, would in part come to explain the many product execution slips and product failures that plagued Craig Barrett's tenure as CEO. Indeed, unlike his successor, Andy Grove had the good fortune to be teamed with Gordon Moore, who was humble enough to face the difficult conditions in the DRAM market, which forced Intel's hand to choose a completely different direction—an all-out focus on driving and meeting the needs of the microprocessor market.

An examination of Intel's history reveals that the pivotal case of abandoning DRAM and focusing on microprocessors led to a *singular* period of *temporary* corporate contrition, when Intel appropriately responded to a strategic inflection point. Not long thereafter, successes resulting from the shift to microprocessors served to reinforce Intel's legendary arrogance, which further fed its "if we build it, they will buy it" attitude toward customers and its "not invented here" aversion to adopting externally developed, best known methods (BKMs). It makes you wonder how many more promising opportunities Intel might have seized if, after being compelled to change this one time, the company had made a habit of being more receptive in its approach to markets, customers, conducting business, and in its treatment of employees.

Once the decision to leave the DRAM business had been made, Andy Grove could get out of the fog, return to familiar ground and give free rein to his unmatched willpower and determination, both of which were needed to convince the organization to start making the shift. What now appears to have been an overnight transformation from this inflection point to a new strategic direction was really a grueling three-year journey.[25] Intel emerged from this journey and subsequently drove Moore's Law with renewed vigor, extending its lead in fab process technology and microprocessor design. As Andy and Intel sharpened their focus to ensure that they would be the very best in the world at realizing Moore's Law with the microprocessor, they also recognized that driving the evolution of manufacturing capability in a growing personal computing industry would mean great financial rewards for the company. Through a combination of technological leadership, growing capacity, and (later) branding, Intel would soon become a global engine driving industry growth. Indeed, with the growth of the sub-$1000 PC industry, Microsoft and Intel became a joined-at-the-hip duopoly (Wintel), and both rode the wave to enormous riches.

There can be no doubt that fab manufacturing played *the* central role in Intel's ascension to these astronomical heights, and it is widely accepted within Intel that Craig Barrett is the one who put Intel's manufacturing house in order in the late 1980s. What's not well known is that *prior* to much of Barrett's success in manufacturing, Will Kauffman, then-vice president of quality assurance, had, over time, developed a deep respect for Japanese manufacturing techniques and had tried repeatedly, without success, to convince Andy Grove that Intel should

---

[25] Andrew S. Grove, *Only the Paranoid Survive* (New York, NY: Doubleday, 1996) 95.

adopt some new (externally developed) manufacturing methods to make the company more competitive. Although Kauffman was eased out of Intel when Barrett was promoted to senior vice president, he did "have the satisfaction of watching Barrett put some of his prescriptions into effect."[26]

What's poignant about this story, though, is that it shows how precedents *against* adhering to the published Intel Values were set, specifically, against risk taking, challenging the status quo, embracing change (even when change is the right thing to do), and listening to all ideas and viewpoints. These behavioral precedents eventually became the *de facto* behavior of managers to subordinates, not only during the Grove years, but also in the subsequent Barrett and Otellini eras. Likewise, the story illustrates another behavioral pattern emerging at the time, whereby an idea that challenges the status quo is eventually embraced, after passing through a period of rejection. Once the idea has been embraced, people who were initially opposed to it can take credit for it, because the true originators of the idea have been forgotten, and have moved on or left the company.

An early and egregious example of this co-opting behavior, which we'll examine in more detail later on, has been described in Tim Jackson's book *Inside Intel,* where it's told that Les Vasdez, a senior manager, got the patent for an invention that fellow manager Federico Faggin had developed before coming to Intel. When Faggin discovered this apparent injustice, he became livid and confronted Andy Grove about it, because Grove was Vasdez's manager. Expecting justice, Faggin instead was turned away by Grove, and he believes that Grove encouraged Vasdez to patent the invention in order to protect Intel's commercial interests, since Faggin had invented it while he was still at Fairchild.[27] Whatever the reason for Grove's actions, they sent out a message that it was acceptable and even encouraged, under certain conditions, to co-opt the work of others. It's interesting to note that this incident took place long before the Intel Values were published, but it helped establish a pattern in the culture of co-opting others' work that would be at variance with making Intel a "Great Place to Work," a Value which calls for "managing performance fairly and firmly." It's no

---

[26] Tim Jackson, *Inside Intel* (New York, NY: Penguin Group, 1997), 297.
[27] Tim Jackson, *Inside Intel* (New York, NY: Penguin Group, 1997), 115-16.

wonder that Faggin left Intel (and went on to start several other companies—a testament to his talent) while Vasdez remained one of Grove's closest confidants.

Andy Grove was a master of details, and when he wanted to know what was really happening within the company, he did not hesitate to investigate via "management by walking around." He understood how to execute his own strategies and directives and, at a minimum, expected the same of his managers, sometimes teetering toward intimidation when they didn't meet his performance expectations. It could be argued that Intel's cultural hallmark of "constructive confrontation" was invented to give license to Andy's management style, which included "in-your-face" intimidation.

**Graphic of Constructive Confrontation**
Image Credit: Miguel Santamarina

The effect of observing a manager's or a leader's behavior is that people will imitate it, and consequently, it was not long before many at Intel would literally be in each other's faces or standing on tables, yelling at each other to get things done. As a result, the culture under Andy Grove became reactive: everyone responded to his or her barking orders, but as patterns of delegation subsequently trickled down through all levels of the organization, people gradually ceased to do things unless their managers told them to. Intimidation from above created a fear in employees that not only prevented them from doing anything without managers' approval, but also created the impetus for avoidance of risks and challenges to the status quo, for fear of manager reprisal at "focal" (the annual performance review cycle).

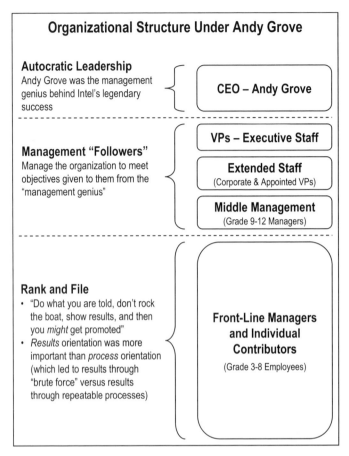

In the Intel of Andy Grove, it was extremely difficult to achieve a healthy balance between a demanding job and personal responsibilities, especially in the early years of the company. People worked long hours in part because they relished the challenges, responsibilities, and clarity of company purpose, but they were also motivated by the rising value of their stock options. In fact, now that they're able to forget the pain of those years, many of Intel's old-timers look on the Andy Grove era as Intel's "golden age", because they long for a return to the time of less ambiguity and an ever-rising stock price. In many ways, these feelings are much like those of a mother whose love for a child and joy in receiving a new addition to the family overshadow the pain of the birthing process. If you were able to endure and survive the stresses of the work environment, you were rewarded handsomely in the form of promotions, pay raises, and stock options, so much so that you became numb or blind to the cultural peculiarities that developed all around you. This numbness or blindness was especially prevalent if Intel was the only point of reference you'd had as a working professional: the behaviors you observed became your model.

And as actions do speak louder than words, these cultural peculiarities—managing upward, ignoring realities, preserving the status quo, co-opting others' ideas or work, utilizing an authoritarian management style—set precedents in the management ranks, which then trickled down to the rank and file of the time. When those rank-and-file personnel were elevated to middle and senior management positions during the 1990s boom years, their dominant behaviors became the DNA of the Intel culture and to this day remain entrenched there, even though they are *inconsistent* with the published company Values. The precedent had already been established (Faggin, Kauffman) for not doing what was "right." Intel values were put in place to establish the right behaviors, but the behavioral precedent had already prevailed (beforehand). Behaviors that would be considered unacceptable and unjust in other companies were accepted and tolerated as long as the stock price kept rising. The destructive effect of these behaviors was apparent only to those with sharp discernment, who could look beyond the high corporate profits and see that gross inefficiencies existed throughout the company, but were masked by monopoly profits.

Under the unambiguous leadership of Andy Grove, when Intel focused on dominating a single, semiconductor market segment—microprocessors—these emerging behaviors had not yet grown to the degree to where they could significantly hurt the company's bottom line, not least because microprocessors were such a profitable focus. However, by the time Intel entered more diverse and competitive (non-CPU) communications markets in the late 1990s, these negative behaviors had incubated long enough to impact Intel's performance. It could certainly be argued that they hindered the development of new product innovations and agile business processes, both of which were needed to effectively compete in the more level playing field outside the company's traditional microprocessor market. When these behaviors—and their consequential impact on Intel's business—are tracked back to Andy Grove's leadership actions, his stature as a so-called management genius can be called into question.

## Evolution of Intel Culture

*Leadership Eras*

Intel had the good fortune to be started by two mature, visionary leaders who knew how to build an egalitarian culture that would lead to outstanding performance. However, within a few short years of this beginning, with Andy Grove's rise to power, the culture became a hybrid in which ideals of cordial egalitarianism and decency struggled against unhealthy doses of paranoia-induced, autocratic action. If an unintended consequence was the institutionalization of cultural behaviors that departed from the founders' ideals but were tolerated for the sake of expediency and a rapidly rising stock price, a more profound effect was the deep familial bond that was forged among employees who collectively experienced the cauldron of the harsh Intel work environment. The survivors thereof were subsequently entitled to a less-stressful existence under Craig Barrett. Continued high revenues and profits, despite a lack of adequate inspection, dulled managerial discernment and further perpetuated the peculiar behaviors (like "gaming") that have become part and parcel of Intel's culture.

Some valuable insights into Intel's leadership under its first three CEOs are provided by Gerry Parker, a retired Intel employee with thirty-two years' service, who personally knew all of them. In 2003, Parker observed that "Bob was clearly the visionary...the symbol of the company, the outside man...looked at by Wall Street investors...Gordon [Moore]...was kind of the strategist and the technologist...that really in my mind set the course for specific technology directions and strategies." Parker views Andy Grove as "the ramrod" who "set the tone for discipline and operational excellence," and further states that Robert Noyce, Gordon Moore, and Andy Grove "complemented each other very well" and that "you needed all three" for Intel to become a success. [28]

---

[28] silicongenesis.stanford.edu/transcripts/parker.htm, Interview with Gerry Parker, October 6, 2003.

In a way, it could be said that Intel's hybrid culture—egalitarian and autocratic—exhibited unusual strength as the company endured hardship and eventually rode a key product innovation from the early years—the microprocessor—into a world-changing power in the late 1980s and beyond. Like a mule, however, this hybrid culture has been stubborn, as evidenced by its failure to successfully adapt to new markets, and since mules cannot procreate, it's worth asking how much longer Intel's culture can survive in its current form before its destructive behaviors erode company performance to the degree that a senior management shakeup is required. As we'll suggest, a better solution may be for the company to improve its performance by returning to the pure egalitarian roots envisioned by its original leaders, Robert Noyce and Gordon Moore, for this would not require such drastic measures.

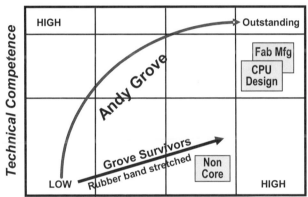

**Ability to Implement Change & Get Results**

## The Era of Growth

In summary, what can be said about Andy Grove as a leader? We cannot argue with Intel's financial results under his leadership. He had a winning combination of technical competence and the discipline of execution. This winning combination is what drove Intel's fab manufacturing and microprocessor design to world-class status. However, he clearly *forced* his style of discipline onto the company, imprinting it with a culture of fear that, as we will see in later chapters, had lasting effects on management and employees once this "force" was no longer present, and which later led to an inefficient bureaucracy.

Clearly, Grove was an amazingly gifted and driven leader who capitalized on a unique set of conditions to make Intel the 800-pound gorilla in the microprocessor market. However, it would also prove to be an amazingly narrow and inflexible juggernaut. Despite dropping an astounding $10 billion on acquisitions, Grove could not set up his successors—nor the company whose culture is largely created in his image—for greater success after his departure as CEO. This criticism doesn't negate the claim of his being the "most influential business person of the last 25 years," but it does call into question the effectiveness and superiority of the Intel culture and its ability to perpetuate superior performance.

VALUES SUMMARY

The leadership actions of Andy Grove exemplified the following Intel Values:

QUALITY

⇒  Achieve the highest standards of excellence
⇒  Do the right things right

GREAT PLACE TO WORK

⇒  Be open and direct
⇒  Recognize and reward accomplishments

DISCIPLINE

⇒  Ensure a safe, clean and injury-free workplace
⇒  Make and meet commitments
⇒  Properly plan, fund and staff projects
⇒  Pay attention to detail

RESULTS ORIENTATION

⇒  Set challenging and competitive goals
⇒  Focus on output
⇒  Assume responsibility
⇒  Constructively confront and solve problems
⇒  Execute flawlessly

BEHAVIORS SUMMARY

The leadership actions of Andy Grove established the *unintended* behaviors:

⇒  Co-opting
⇒  Preserving the status quo
⇒  Managing upward
⇒  Ignoring realities
⇒  "In your face," bullying management style

# Chapter 2

# Leadership from the Trenches

> The world is divided into people who do things, and people who get the credit. Try, if you can, to belong to the first class. There's far less competition.[29]
>
> Dwight Morrow

In early 2005, near the end of his tenure as CEO, Craig Barrett proclaimed that the health of Intel's culture could be gauged by the performance of Intel's products, because "product performance cannot lie." On the surface, this seems like a good measure of corporate health and one that any Intel manager would eagerly point to because, for most of its history, Intel has been a clear leader when it comes to the performance of its microprocessor products. However, against the backdrop of a diverse corporation comprising several different functional groups, product performance, while vitally important, arguably does not provide an adequate *universal* measure of corporate cultural health. Indeed, the work or output of several organizations within Intel has little direct bearing on product performance, so the cultural health of such organizations cannot accurately be correlated to product performance. On the other hand, product performance *is* a good way (but not the only way) to measure the cultural health of those organizations or areas heavily involved in the design and manufacture of Intel's products—especially those whose core competencies have become competitive advantages for Intel. Two such areas come to mind: Intel's development of fab process technology and its microprocessor design.

In this chapter we will look at some of the key features of Intel's

---

culture within the domains of its fab process technology and microprocessor design teams, specifically the P6 microprocessor design team. As we will discover, the behaviors practiced within these areas are highly consistent with the published Intel Values, a fact that, coupled with the historically stellar performance of Intel's microprocessors, would lead one to conclude that the culture within these organizations is indeed healthy. Moreover, a study of these two areas provides insights against which we can contrast the rest of Intel, in order to gauge the overall health of the company's culture. It is only through such an examination that we can (1) come to more fully appreciate the practices that led to Intel's technological and market leadership and (2) better understand the predominant culture that exists outside of these two areas of core competency at Intel.

## The Moore's Law Express

Intel's obsession with and leadership in the microprocessor market can be traced back to 1965, three years prior to the company's founding, when Gordon Moore articulated what was later to become known as Moore's Law. He had observed that, from the days of the original planar transistor back in 1959, the industry had in every year doubled the number of transistors that could be put on a chip. Ten years later he revised his prediction, stating that this doubling would take place every twenty-four months, not once every year. Since 1975 this prediction has been amazingly accurate, and exponential increases in the number of transistors in Intel microprocessor products have been the embodiment of this law. In true visionary fashion, Moore had discerned and articulated the underlying pattern of integrated circuit development, a pattern that would drive an entire industry for decades to come.

In the early days of Intel, long before the emergence of its exclusive focus on driving the microprocessor business, the company's core competencies consisted of silicon design and process technology innovation. By virtue of their reputations, Robert Noyce and Gordon Moore were able to attract the most talented engineers from throughout the industry, who were willing to take pay cuts and lower-level positions just to be a part of the exciting new company started by these two Silicon Valley icons. With abundant talent in-house, Intel soon became a high-tech leader with three great product innovations during its first ten years.

These innovations were DRAM, erasable programmable read-only memory (EPROM), and the microprocessor—the product upon which Intel's greatest success would rest. All three of these were *significant* design innovations in the electronics industry and led to the development of great products, most notably the personal computer. Notwithstanding these significant achievements, after ten years in business, Intel was still an immature company in the international arena and faced increasing competition from larger, better-financed Japanese manufacturers.

When Andy Grove and Gordon Moore made their monumental mid 1980s decision to exit the DRAM business, the resulting focus on the microprocessor market gave new birth to Intel's passion for using its technological leadership to drive Moore's Law within the microprocessor business. The results were legendary, as Intel's technological lead, coupled with its ever-expanding factory capacity and a masterful "Intel Inside" brand campaign, created a multi-layered fortress of competitive advantage that enabled Intel to dominate the microprocessor market and drive out nearly all its competition.

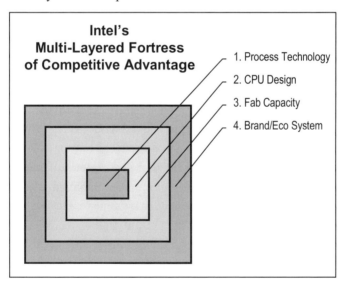

While it's true that each layer in this fortress played an important part in Intel's overall strategy, by the mid 1990s it would become clear that its *technological leadership in fab process technology and microprocessor design* would be the most distinct and difficult features for competitors to copy. Intel's passionate and successful advancement of Moore's Law would soon become an unstoppable high-speed train, which we'll call the "Moore's Law Express," because it created the further momentum that enabled Intel to garner monopoly profits as its stock soared to astronomical levels.

## Fab Manufacturing Process Technology

It was very clear from Andy Grove's research that the crown jewels of Intel manufacturing were tied to Moore's Law. This relationship between manufacturing and Moore's Law has proven itself during the boom years of the PC industry where the silicon requirements were simple, with low-mix high-volume products that could be pumped through the Intel fab behemoth.

No one can truly appreciate the number of patents that have gone into the development of Intel's fab process technology. Nor can anyone fully appreciate the amount of money it has invested in capital equipment. If you've ever been inside an Intel fab, you will begin to realize where all its money has gone. The Intel fab network is one of the most high-tech, sophisticated silicon-producing "machines" in the world. It hums like a well-tuned Ferrari. When the Intel fab is at peak capacity, it supplies the world with microprocessors. This is an amazing feat, considering that the scale of process technology at 90 nanometers[30] now approaches that of DNA inside the human cell. This is a remarkable accomplishment for a company that is only thirty-eight years old.

An examination of the practices within Intel's fab environment helps to explain how Intel was able to achieve such impressive results with its process technology. Most prominent among these practices are (1) selective hiring to ensure technical competence, (2) effective development and use of new technologies, and (3) process orientation along with a focus on incremental improvement. These three practices formed a synergistic relationship that drove process improvements and breakthroughs.

The "rite of passage" into fab was first and foremost a degree in chemical engineering (theory). From there, people were given additional training in statistics, yield management, process technology, and other fields representing the experiential attributes of technical competence. Education did not end here, but was a continuous process dictated by the

---

[30] A nanometer is a unit of spatial measurement that is $10^{-9}$ meter, or one billionth of a meter.

precepts of Moore's Law. Everyone—from the technicians operating machines to the project managers overseeing silicon development and validation—had to be at the top of their game in order to drive the next generation of manufacturing process technology. Since Intel's fortunes were derived from fab process technology, having clear project ownership, authority, and accountability were paramount to driving successive generations of more efficient and effective chip-manufacturing capabilities.

Likewise, much of Intel's success was based on its ability to pioneer the use of its new technologies in the development and manufacture of its complex products. During his final years as CEO, Craig Barrett was fond of saying that Intel built the most complex products known to humanity—a claim easily supported by the fact that Intel's most complex microprocessors contain more than one billion transistors. Again, one could add the claim that Intel's skillful and passionate development and use of manufacturing process technology played *the* vital role in supporting this complexity and advancing Moore's Law. Indeed, Intel has not only been a great pioneer of technologies that directly support its core competency, but it has also successfully partnered with and leveraged the skills of dozens of capital equipment vendors to help develop many of these technologies.

Intel has proceeded very methodically in advancing its fab processes. Each successive generation of its technology builds on the previous one, relying on lower-risk incremental steps instead of high-risk strategic leaps. For example, when the process technology advances from one generation to the next, several of the numerous equipment modules designed for the current generation are made capable of supporting the next. That way, Intel doesn't need to change *all* the equipment in the line, but rather can focus only on those pieces that will not support the next generation. Even though the progression can be characterized as a series of coordinated, incremental steps rather than a strategic leap, overall, the result might be more of a leap than an incremental step.

When a new piece of equipment is required for a particular module within the line, Intel has at its disposal several options to satisfy the requirement. For example, Intel can

- set up head-to-head competition among competing vendors to produce new equipment to meet its needs,

- make suggestions to an existing vendor on how a particular piece of equipment could be improved to meet Intel-specific requirements, or
- design an entirely new piece of equipment and have an equipment vendor manufacture it.

In nearly all cases, Intel can further extend its competitive advantage in process technology. Whenever new equipment and technologies are developed for Intel's specific requirements, the vendors are generally prohibited from selling them to other customers (like AMD) for a given period, thus giving Intel exclusive access to that newly developed technology. Intel is getting the best of both worlds; it's able to combine its own in-house skills with those of its equipment vendors to develop technologies that support its core competency, and at the same time, it can keep most of these developments for its exclusive use until products are launched into the market. Each intra- and inter-generational improvement to fab manufacturing processes accelerates Intel's technological lead, and at the same time reduces its manufacturing costs by 25 to 30% per year (as depicted in the graphic below).

## The Cost Reduction Engine

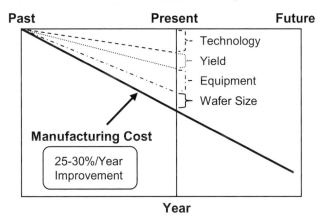

Much of Intel's quest to perpetually improve fab process technology can be attributed to Gordon Moore's belief that "Only by processing large numbers of wafers through the same fab under the same process…could you make the improvements that allowed you to cut your costs."[31] This disciplined process orientation, coupled with the focused development and application of key enabling technologies, left Intel's competitors farther and farther behind. As manufacturing processes improved, so did product yields, which resulted in more sellable products and higher revenue and profit margins; these in turn provided increased funding to support more capital equipment investments, leading to increased capacity (wafer and die size) and further improvements to fab process technology. So went the Intel's technology flywheel from the late 1980s through the 1990s, leading to its domination of the industry.

## P6 Design Team

Along with Intel's unmatched leadership in fab manufacturing and process technology, the P6[32] project team provides another excellent example of Intel at its best. Among the many microprocessor design teams in Intel's history, the P6 project team stands head and shoulders above the rest. Launched in 1990, this team developed Intel's sixth-generation x86[33] microprocessor architecture, which replaced the original Pentium design. In 1995, the Pentium Pro became the first P6-based microprocessor to be released; it was followed by an impressive string of subsequent microprocessors based on the P6 core, including the Pentium II, Pentium III, and the Pentium M, the heart of Intel's highly successful Centrino mobile platform. [34]

As with all microprocessor development teams at Intel, the P6 team was under tremendous pressure to create a next-generation design that would further Moore's Law for the next several years. The P6 design would have to be *significantly* more powerful than the P5 or Pentium design. In this respect, the P6 team did not disappoint, as their design proved to be highly efficient and scalable. In fact, the later versions of P6 chips performed so well that Intel had a difficult time gaining market

---

[31] Tim Jackson, *Inside Intel* (New York, NY: Penguin Group, 1997), 250.

[32] Because one cannot establish trademark rights on numbers, Intel and most of its competitors began to use trademark-acceptable names such as *P*entium for subsequent generations of processors.

[33] The architecture is called x86 because the earliest processors in this family were identified by model numbers ending in the sequence "86": the 8086, the 80186, the 80286, the 386, and the 486.

[34] The following microprocessors are based on the P6 core: Celeron (Pentium II/III Derivative), Celeron M (Banias Derivative), Pentium Pro, Pentium II, Pentium II Xeon, Pentium III, Pentium III Xeon, and Pentium M.

acceptance for its subsequent x86 microarchitecture (NetBurst) offerings when they were released in 2000. Perhaps there's no better tribute to the P6 team than the fact that the next generation has not been able to completely displace P6-based chips. To this day, and amazingly so, microprocessors derived from the work of the P6 project team are still the main source of Intel's revenues! Indeed, no microprocessor development effort before or since has come close to matching the P6 team's success.

When you consider that achievement in the celebrated history of Intel, you have to ask, "What were the significant factors that made this team so outstanding?" The answers to this question will make perfect sense to any objective reader, yet it will be seen that they differ from many practices and behaviors that predominate in Intel's culture today. For instance, the first employee assigned to the P6 project was a recently hired outsider, Robert P. Colwell, whose first job at Intel was "senior computer architect" for the project. [35] This hiring and project assignment represented a significant departure from Intel's "promote from within" philosophy, and yet it proved to be one of the best decisions the company would make, as it brought a needed fresh perspective to the challenges of creating the next generation x86 microarchitecture. Indeed, in his book *The Pentium Chronicles*, Colwell describes in detail the phases of this landmark project and points out that "the P6 project was blessed with a team whose members either had never worked on Intel's x86 chips or had never worked at Intel. This helped enormously in getting the right balance of historical answers and new challenges."[36] Getting "the right balance" of inside and outside knowledge and experience onto the P6 team fomented the level of creativity needed to catapult x86 microprocessor design to the next level. This was just one of several key factors that led to the project's success. Other factors included:

1. <u>Rigorous assessment and assignment of personnel</u>. The P6 project team faced the daunting task of managing rapid growth in the project's complexity and in the size of the team itself as it grew into a division consisting of thousands of employees. Colwell repeatedly pays tribute to Randy Steck, the P6 design

---

[35] Robert P. Colwell, *The Pentium Chronicles* (Hoboken, New Jersey: John Wiley & Sons, Inc., 2006), 1.
[36] Ibid, 6.

manager (and future division general manager and vice president), who possessed an innate ability to successfully work through these difficult challenges. Steck displayed an amazing ability to look beyond the typical threshold measures of competence (a given academic degree) in order to judge how to make the best use of an engineer's individual gifts and interests. Such detailed assessment and assignment of personnel led to the creation of the most effective team possible.[37]

2. <u>Seeking and adopting BKMs and learning from mistakes</u>.[38] It's somewhat ironic that amidst Intel's "not invented here" culture, it was an engineering design team that fully sought and embraced BKMs in lieu of wasting precious time and energy reinventing the wheel. Of all Intel personnel, engineers had the most justification for clinging to the "not invented here" mentality and rejecting external BKMs, yet the P6 team displayed a level of humility that's uncommon at Intel, as they endeavored to learn from mistakes and adopt proven BKMs.

3. <u>Absence of egos while possessing a strong orientation to detail</u>. Colwell mentions that he enjoyed the P6 project so much because the five lead architects "avoided ego clashes"[39] and were willing to dive into the details with each other and with the design teams in order to make sure difficult issues were resolved.

4. <u>Being data-driven doers rather than mere talkers</u>. The team took measures to quash talkers who "generate endless streams of rhetoric that…[bring] you no closer to resolving anything," because they knew that "there is no religious demagogue worse that an engineer arguing from intuition instead of data." Instead, the team established a data-driven culture of doers, to which Colwell attributes timely decisions on key design issues in the early stages of the project. [40]

5. <u>Utilizing small sub-teams and avoiding bureaucracy</u>. A large project team such as the P6 has an endless list of tasks that must be completed. Nearly all of this work must be assigned to

---

[37] Ibid, 34-35.
[38] Ibid, 6, 44.
[39] Ibid, 16.
[40] Ibid, 19, 20.

numerous sub-teams whose work must be coordinated. The P6 team was careful to make sure that the number of people on most sub-teams did not exceed ten in order to keep them nimble and action-oriented.[41] Furthermore, many of these sub-teams rolled up through the lead architects, and not their usual management chains, in order to streamline communication and decision making. Pointing out that the overall size of the P6 team was much smaller than that of the NetBurst team, which was led by marketing engineers who loved to hold meetings and make presentations, Colwell hints that the added size and bureaucracy of the NetBurst team no doubt contributed to its less-significant results.[42] Perhaps one little experience demonstrates the P6 team's disdain for bureaucracy better than any other. In the early days of the project, when there was a crying need for a dedicated conference room though none was to be found, the architects took over a large, under-utilized storage room—without seeking permission through normal channels (the Intel bureaucracy) because they believed it was easier to ask forgiveness than to get permission.[43]

It should come as no surprise that most of these practices and behaviors are consistent with the published Intel Values. Nor should it be a surprise that these practices and behaviors are consistent with those found in the fab manufacturing culture of Intel, because design and manufacturing had to be interdependent to achieve success on the "Moore's Law Express." If a culture's health and strength are determined by the alignment between its published values (ideology) and actual behaviors, then it could be said that the cultures of the P6 design team and fab process technology development groups were quite strong. Moreover, there can be little doubt that the groups' behavioral culture led directly to Intel's dominance in the PC industry, hence to its phenomenal earnings growth and the meteoric rise of its stock price.

## The Moore's Law Express Money Machine

While developers of fab process technology and the P6 design team

---

[41] Ibid, 50.
[42] Ibid, 51-52.
[43] Ibid, 18.

together built the "Moore's Law Express," many other groups at Intel took these accomplishments for granted. An unintended consequence of the Moore's Law Express was the masking and subsidizing of incompetence in non-core functional areas and anomalous behaviors that are now inconsistent with the published Intel Values. Many of these non-core areas were augmented by increasing headcount and gluing together ad hoc processes that would not detract from the performance of the Moore's Law Express. In essence, the job of these functional areas was to "not hurt" the company while achieving the requirement of meeting the worldwide microprocessor demand. Generally, speaking, personnel in these ancillary, non-core areas, when compared to those developing fab process technology and designing microprocessors, were woefully lacking in terms of a process orientation and the technical competence to continuously improve operations.

The manufacturing model for advancing Moore's Law was directly tied to advancing the performance of chips based on clock speed. This model became predictive and afforded Intel the advantage of knowing what was required to develop next-generation capital equipment to support subsequent manufacturing processes. The core competency in fab process technology became the cost-reduction engine that eventually made computing affordable to the masses. This engine served Intel well throughout the 1980s and 1990s, until the PC market in the developed world reached maturity. Up until that time, corporate customers and individual consumers had been riding the wave of a new PC industry that helped spawn the Internet. After "year 2000," the world changed, and these same customers began to require different microprocessor capabilities to fulfill their voracious appetites for greater productivity and personal recreation in the fascinating digital world.

**VALUES SUMMARY**

The actions of key personnel in fab manufacturing process development and P6 design team exemplified the following Intel Values:

**DISCIPLINE**

⇒ Make and meet commitments

⇒ Properly plan, fund and staff projects

⇒ Pay attention to detail

**QUALITY**

⇒ Achieve the highest standards of excellence

⇒ Do the right things right

**RISK TAKING**

⇒ Foster innovation and creative thinking

⇒ Listen to all ideas and viewpoints

**GREAT PLACE TO WORK**

⇒ Be open and direct

⇒ Recognize and reward accomplishments

⇒ Work as a team with respect and trust for each other

⇒ Promote a challenging work environment that develops our workforce

**RESULTS ORIENTATION**

⇒ Set challenging and competitive goals

⇒ Focus on output

⇒ Constructively confront and solve problems

⇒ Execute flawlessly

**BEHAVIORS SUMMARY**

⇒ Seeking outside talent to challenge the status quo

⇒ Differentiating personnel based on level of technical competence, putting the right people into the right positions

⇒ Strong detail orientation where data drive the decisions and actions

# Chapter 3

# Andy's Gone, Now What?

The gap nobody knows is the gap between what a company's leaders want to achieve and the ability of their organization to achieve it.[44]

Larry Bossidy

In May of 1998, under deceptively challenging circumstances, Craig Barrett became CEO at the world's largest semiconductor company. Intel still held a dominant position in the PC microprocessor market, but profits were down significantly from the previous year: Intel's competitors were taking market share—especially in the sub-$1,000 PC market known as segment zero; the PC market was showing signs of reaching maturation; and finally, Barrett had the unenviable task of following a legend like Andy Grove while being subject to the inevitable pressures of continuing Intel's growth.

Barrett had been a Stanford professor when he first joined Intel in 1973, but he had left after a year, citing as his reason Intel's "crazy environment," a highly political and fear-driven culture that bred arrogance into those who survived it.[45] Immediately after leaving Intel and returning to Stanford, he realized that he had "probably made a dumb decision," so six months later he returned to Intel for good.[46]

Until Barrett's arrival at Intel, the quality of the company's products had been below standard. Barrett instituted statistical process control into

---

[44] Larry Bossidy and Ram Charan, *Execution: The Discipline of Getting Things Done* (New York, NY: Crown Business, 2002), 19.
[45] The 'Barrett Traverse,' *Newsweek*. New York: April 20, 1998. Vol. 131, Iss. 16, pg. 46.
[46] Ibid.

the manufacturing arena for all factories worldwide, which was no easy task, as it meant teaching everyone statistics and quality methods. Barrett's success with this assignment put him at the forefront of Intel's leadership pipeline and led him to ever-increasing roles of responsibility, until eventually he became CEO.

The dramatic earnings- and stock-price-growth Intel had experienced after the exodus of CEOs Noyce and Moore did not recur in the Barrett era following the departure of Andy Grove. Rather, the company continued to live off the microprocessor cash cow that was established under Grove's leadership. It has been argued that great leaders set their successors up for even greater success; however, it would take a huge leap of faith to say that Andy Grove set up Craig Barrett for success, because a look at the stock performance suggests otherwise.

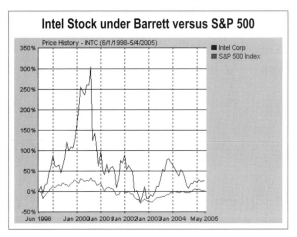

If Barrett's effectiveness as CEO is judged by stock-price performance, it is clear that Barrett falls well short of Andy Grove's stellar record. As seen in the chart above,[47] Intel's stock price performed only marginally better than the Standard & Poor's Composite Index (S&P 500) from June 1998 through May 2005, the Craig Barrett era. During the first two years of his tenure, the stock significantly outperformed the S&P 500, probably because of the continued momentum from the Grove era, a "pop" in the PC market in anticipation of the "Y2K" problem (fear of mass computer failures at the turn of the millennium), and widespread stock-price inflation during the Internet

---

[47] moneycentral.msn.com

bubble. When that bubble burst, nearly all of the post-1998 gains in Intel's stock price were lost, and the stock subsequently tracked more closely to the S&P 500. By this measure alone—the fact that Intel did not significantly outperform the index during the Barrett era—it would appear that Intel could no longer be considered a growth company.

Interestingly, when Intel's internal news website ran an article in 2005 reflecting on Barrett's tenure as CEO, it chose to highlight the five-fold increase in the value of the Intel brand, but omitted any reference to stock-price performance—a measurement of value that is far more important to Intel employees and shareholders than "brand value," but one by which Barrett's performance fared less well. At least one analyst suggested that Barrett "should be removed [as Chairman of the Board], since he presided over such terrible decision making and lack of shareholder value creation for his entire tenure as CEO."[48]

So how could Intel go from a dominant position in the PC market at the time of the Grove-Barrett transition to its current position, where it is losing CPU market share to AMD and has nothing to show for the $10 billion it spent on acquisitions in the late 1990s and early 2000s? The authors believe that by looking more deeply into the transition in leadership from Andy Grove to Craig Barrett, we can provide a multi-dimensional and revealing analysis of Intel to help outsiders appreciate the evolution of the culture and understand why company performance has been so lackluster in recent years.

At the beginning of 1998, Intel's CPU product line was very simple. By the end of that year, Intel had segmented its offerings by introducing products aimed at specific markets: Xeon chips for servers, Pentium for desktops, and Celeron to do battle with the likes of AMD and Cyrix in the bargain PC market. This simple change of segmenting the CPU product line introduced myriad complexities into Intel's fragile business process environment and contributed to the massive increase in personnel needed to handle the complexity. Product segmentation is just one of many examples that could be cited to show how Intel changed significantly during the transition in leadership from Grove to Barrett, creating exponentially greater challenges for Barrett and the rest of the company. Additional dimensions of change during this transition,

---

[48] Bernstein Research, INTC and AMD: Part IV – Management Decisions and What To Do Now, March 13, 2006.

including market, leadership, and culturally driven factors, are summarized in the table below.

| Dimension | Grove (to 1998) | Barrett (by 2000) |
|---|---|---|
| CPU Product Line | Simple | Segmented, complex |
| Focus of Growth | Chase CPU demand | Diversification |
| Strategy/Execution | G. Moore/A. Grove | A. Grove/C. Barrett |
| Management Style | In-your-face, do what I say, "follow me" leadership | Non-confrontational, invoke the spirit of the Values |
| Employee Mindset (how to get ahead) | Survive (servile delivery of expected results) | Manage upward to become entitled |
| Headcount | 65,000 | 86,000 |
| Discipline | Imposed or forced by authoritarian leadership | Lack of discipline (rubber band discipline) |
| Results | Expected *and* inspected | Expected but *not* inspected |
| Decision making and Accountability | Clear with rewards or consequences based on results | Lost in bureaucracy and "spinning" of results |

## Focus of Growth

For most of Andy Grove's tenure as CEO, the focus of growth for Intel was straightforward: create and chase the CPU demand. One former Intel employee summed up this strategy as follows:

> Make sure the customer has only one source for CPU junk, and make sure that it underperforms the current offerings from our partner in duopolistic cheatery (Microsoft) such that said customer will perpetually require newer and slightly faster junk.[49]

While this viewpoint is highly cynical, it does have a ring of truth.

---

[49]http://messages.finance.yahoo.com/Business_%26_Finance/Investments/Sectors/Techn ology/Semiconductors/threadview?bn=9609&tid=848810&mid=848810

Intel was able to keep product performance one step ahead of the competition in order to preserve its market share, without getting so far ahead that customers would lack an incentive to frequently upgrade their PCs. Due to the fierce competition among the PC original equipment manufacturers (OEMs) and the fact that Intel was the sole supplier of leading-edge microprocessors for these OEMs, Intel was able to garner a disproportionately high share of the profits in the PC supply chain. This strategy worked amazingly well from the release of the 386 chip until the advent of the sub-$1,000 PC market in 1998, when Intel was caught off guard by the popularity of products in that segment—products that met the vast majority of consumers' basic computing needs (email, word processing, Internet browsing, etc.).

Fortunately for Intel, the introduction of Xeon server chips in 1998 provided a product line with very high margins to compensate for the falling average selling prices in the consumer PC segment. Intel was also able to improve manufacturing efficiencies such that it could lower product costs and regain most of the market share it had lost to AMD and Cyrix in what Grove termed "segment zero."[50]

Notwithstanding these gains in its share of the growing sub-$1000 PC market and the growth in the x86 server market, Intel's leaders sought to diversify the company beyond microprocessors so that revenues and profits would continue growing and keep the stock price on its ever-upward trend. In Intel's 2000 annual report, Andy Grove and Craig Barrett discussed Intel's vision for growth through the Internet transition, a vision that included acquisitions and organic diversification. Barrett stated that Intel would continue to make most of its revenue—roughly 80%—from selling CPUs, specifically the Intel Architecture Group (IAG)'s microprocessors, chipsets, and motherboards (its core business), but he also emphasized that the company needed to grow revenues outside of its core business. Indeed, Intel was trying to position itself as "the building block supplier to the Internet economy."

When discussing the execution requirements to meet this bold vision, Andy Grove acknowledged that Intel would have to "ramp up our execution skills to keep up with the demands of the more complex product markets that we're serving now. The demands on operational

---

[50] Grove, Andrew S. "Managing Segment Zero," *Leader to Leader*, 11 (Winter 1999): 16-21. http://www.pfdf.org/leaderbooks/L2L/winter99/grove.html.

excellence have increased at a time when operations are tougher, broader, and more diverse than ever before." Barrett agreed with Grove's assessment, adding that despite the increased complexity year after year, "people still expect the same performance from Intel, and we intend to deliver it."[51]

Both Grove and Barrett realized that additional product lines and market complexity—closely linked with Intel's acquisition strategy— would really test Intel's ability to execute. What they did not realize, or at least explicitly articulate, were some of the specific challenges Intel would have to overcome in order to be successful outside of its core business.

1. <u>More Competition</u> – Intel was entering markets that were uncharted territory—networking and communications. It would be starting at the bottom in terms of market share and would have to compete on a more level playing field than it was accustomed to with microprocessor products.

2. <u>Less Focus, More Funding</u> – As product scope increased dramatically by virtue of the acquisitions and new internal product development, the natural result was less organizational focus, and more importantly, the need to fund everything instead of focusing on key markets or customer segments.

3. <u>Capability Mismatch</u> – When attempting to assimilate the organizations it had acquired, Intel became acutely aware that its advantages in semiconductor design and manufacturing were very specific to microprocessor products, and that the leadership would have to change and learn how to compete.

4. <u>New Hires</u> – As headcount grew by a whopping 33% between 1998 and 2000, Intel had the daunting task of acculturating thousands of new employees, many of whom came as a result of acquisitions and were bumping up against a microprocessor business model that was not adaptable to these new markets.

5. <u>Complacency</u> – Finally, Intel's wild success or "rising tide" had "lifted all the boats" in the late '80s and early '90s. In the later 1990s, as demand for microprocessors softened, personnel were "punching the clock," watching the ever-rising stock price and

---

[51] Intel's 2000 Annual Report

becoming complacent with their many stock options. This marked a sea-change from the mid 1980s, when Intel had struggled to recover from getting crushed in the DRAM market, and employees had frenetically adapted to the voracious demand of the PC market.

By the end of 2004, it became clear that Intel had not performed well in addressing these challenges and reaching its stated goals of growing non-IAG revenues beyond 20% of the corporate total. Despite the $10 billion poured into non-core business acquisitions to boost growth, Intel's non-IAG revenue had actually fallen to only 14.7% of total corporate revenues. From an employee standpoint, moreover, no apparent plan had been put forth by management on how these goals would be met; there had been a lot of vision, but no concrete plans for execution.

In summary, the focus of Intel's growth changed significantly in the brief span of years marking the leadership transition from Andy Grove to Craig Barrett. From a relatively *simple* CPU-dominated product line before 1998, Intel moved to a *complex,* multi-segment CPU product line in 1998, and then rapidly expanded into complex communications and networking silicon product lines after 1998. Under Andy Grove, Intel had been able to execute a simple growth strategy; under Craig Barrett, the company was less successful in executing a more complex strategy.

## Strategy and Execution

In conjunction with changes in growth strategy that occurred during the leadership transition years, it's worth comparing some key actions of the Grove-Barrett (Chairman-CEO) tandem during this acquisition binge, with those of the Moore-Grove tandem during the earlier (mid 1980s) inflection point, when the latter led Intel out of DRAM and into microprocessors. The circumstances leading to the acquisition strategy in the late 1990s were not nearly as dire as those Gordon Moore and Andy Grove had faced many years earlier, when the very existence of Intel was seriously threatened. Clearly, the impetus behind the acquisition strategy was a desire for continued growth, with the hope being that new silicon products would serve as "building blocks" for the Internet economy. As a participant in expansive networking and communications markets, Intel could grow revenues and earnings in order to keep the stock on its continual upward spiral.

Hence Intel proceeded with its aggressive acquisition strategy, though it appeared to many inside observers as a "shotgun" approach, in an attempt to create momentum outside of its core business. Curiously, Craig Barrett never communicated any specific financial goals for assimilating the acquisitions into the Intel Communications Group (ICG), but he did say, "we continue to drive the convergence of computing and communications through our product lineup, and with this we see wireless local-area networking and wide-area cellular technologies coming together."[52] There was no comment on the hundreds of millions in operating losses or the $600 million write-down of goodwill on the acquisitions.[53]

| Operating Income for ICG (Acquisitions) | | | | |
|---|---|---|---|---|
| 2000 | 2001 | 2002 | 2003 | 2004 |
| $   319 | $   (735) | $   (817) | $   (824) | $   (791) |

Taken from Intel Annual Reports, 2000-2004

Intel's personnel and recruiting strategy for the acquisitions was not distinguished by piercing insights like Gordon Moore's earlier recognition of the need for existing executives and employees to change their areas of knowledge and expertise in order to remain with the company. Rather, it's common knowledge that the prevailing attitude was to run the acquisitions like the CPU business: in other words, to "share" Intel BKMs (best known methods) with these smaller, ostensibly less-sophisticated businesses in order to make them market leaders. You could almost hear senior management saying, "Who better than our own 'proven' managers to take the lead?" Perhaps such a thought process would explain why key positions were filled primarily by unqualified "Grove Survivors"—seemingly as a reward for long service to Intel—in what appeared to be an *entitlement* rather than a robust process of matching job requirements with candidate competencies. The Intel arrogance served only to drive out the talent from these acquisitions.

Because the acquisition strategy failed, we may never know what discussions took place during its formation and execution. Nor do we

---

[52] John G. Spooner, "Intel to combine networking chip groups,"
http://news.com.com/Intel+to+combine+networking+chip+groups/2100-1039_3-5118962.html
[53] Ibid.

know what individual roles Grove, Barrett, and possibly Moore played during this transition. In the minds of most Intel employees—and, more recently, in the eyes of the press—it appears that Craig Barrett is to blame for this strategy's failure. However, a deeper look reveals plenty of evidence to suggest that Andy Grove is equally, if not more, responsible for Intel's inability to succeed in its diversification push.

We need look no further than Intel's departure from the DRAM market (when Gordon Moore was Chairman) to see historical precedents for the chairman's role as chief strategist among the Intel leaders. That this remained the case during Intel's diversification seems apparent from a January 1999 *Business Week* article that refers to the "combination of Grove, who spins Intel's vision, and Barrett, who executes with cool precision," implying that when it comes to vision and strategy formulation, the chairman, Andy Grove, took the lead.[54] Finally, in a January 2001 Intel Communications article, Andy Grove is quoted as saying "There are no acquisitions that I wish we hadn't made. No choices that I have regretted. None of the acquisitions have run into major organizational or integration problems. All are becoming valuable parts of Intel. So the strategy seems right and the execution seems right." Whether or not Andy was the one who eventually "pulled the trigger" on these acquisitions, his comments make it clear that he was fully behind the strategy. Over the final two years of the Barrett era, it seemed that Intel was quietly trying to sweep the acquisition strategy under the rug, as a thing of the distant past. But this whole foray into new markets provides valuable insights into the behaviors characterizing Intel culture and helps us gauge the effectiveness of Intel's leaders, past and present. For example, one plausible interpretation of the failed acquisition strategy would be to view Barrett as a devoted "follower" who was merely trying to execute the desires of his predecessor, Grove. Although Craig Barrett is an extremely intelligent Stanford PhD, it is reasonable to ask whether he questioned the acquisition strategy, not in terms of its strategic importance, but rather in terms of whether it was feasible for Intel to execute that strategy, given its manufacturing focus on microprocessors and the dearth of appropriate skills among long-time Intel managers. What we propose is that Craig Barrett, upon becoming CEO, abdicated the execution of the acquisition strategy by delegating it

---

[54] "The Top 25 Executives of the Year," *Business Week*, 11 January 1999, 58-80.

to subordinates, without inspecting progress in Grove-like fashion to ensure that the expected results were being achieved. (This assumes that some expected results were communicated in the senior management ranks.)

Although Craig Barrett continued the investment trend in fab manufacturing, he did not foresee nor did he yield—even at the behest of the P6 design leadership—to the emerging market trends in CPU design that were moving toward a low-power/performance vector.[55] Thus, by the end of Barrett's tenure in 2005, Intel's leadership in CPUs had suffered to the extent that, instead of being "one generation ahead" in microprocessor design, Intel was "one generation behind."[56] These execution missteps support our premise that leaders need a winning combination of technical competence and the discipline of execution; they also indicate that Craig Barrett fell short on the latter, especially when it came to *inspecting* management behaviors and holding managers accountable for results as well as adherence to the Intel Values.

In contrast to Andy Grove's detailed and demanding modus operandi, Craig Barrett did not appear to set clear goals and priorities for the acquisitions. It's not clear, for example, whether Intel made those acquisitions to secure intellectual property only, to enter new markets, or merely to eliminate potential competition in those markets. Nor did Barrett follow through on how those companies were assimilating and progressing toward goals. When product introductions were delayed, Barrett frequently invoked the Intel Values in the hopes of improving company performance. However, in the eyes of many employees who pointed to the need to "clean out" what they saw as a bureaucracy filled with sycophantic managers who repeatedly violated those Values, Barrett's tough words regarding adherence to Intel Values were not accompanied by tough actions. This one discrepancy—the gap between his expectations and the lack of actual results—testifies to Barrett's inability or unwillingness to follow through in rewarding and punishing people's behaviors as appropriate. Based on his failure to enforce the Intel Values and perpetuate disciplined execution in the management

---

[55] Robert P. Colwell, *The Pentium Chronicles* (Hoboken, New Jersey: John Wiley & Sons, Inc., 2006), 167-168. Colwell doesn't implicate Barrett directly, but he mentions that he could not get "anyone" in senior management at Intel to listen to his urging to address thermal dissipation and the changing market requirements for CPUs.

[56] "One Generation Ahead" was one of Barrett's hallmark initiatives at Intel.

ranks he inherited from Andy Grove, it would appear that Craig Barrett was essentially an ineffective caretaker CEO.

The graphic below summarizes Craig Barrett's leadership era: continued investment in fab manufacturing leadership, decline in CPU design leadership, extreme growth in bureaucracy, and ineffectiveness in non-core functional areas. It was this growth in bureaucracy that would cast a shadow on Barrett's tenure, as the culture transitioned to one of entitlement, living off the fruits of the core competencies established under Andy Grove.

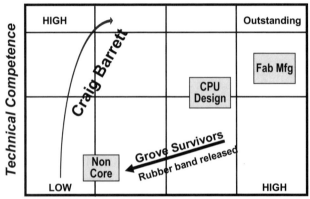

### The Era of Entitlement

As Intel prepared for the CEO transition from Craig Barrett to Paul Otellini in 2005, both the press and Intel's internal news website were full of stories about the impending transfer of power. In many of the stories, monikers were attached to each of Intel's CEOs: Robert Noyce was labeled "the ultimate entrepreneur," Gordon Moore "the brilliant engineer," Andy Grove "the industry visionary" and "management genius," Craig Barrett "the manufacturing hero," and Paul Otellini the self-described "product guy."

If Craig Barrett had been asked back in 2000 what he wanted his moniker to be when he stepped down as CEO, one wonders whether he would have said something like *"the great diversifier"* of Intel, who grew company revenue and profits through skillful execution of his bold acquisition strategy. One could speculate that because of this strategy's failure, Barrett had to be given another label in media stories about Intel's leadership transition. Thus, hearkening back to the work of his pre-CEO leadership within Intel's manufacturing group and recognizing the investments he made in manufacturing while CEO, Barrett was called "the manufacturing hero" who built Intel into a global manufacturing powerhouse.

When we compare the vision and execution capabilities of the Gordon Moore-Andy Grove tandem (with Grove as CEO) in the mid 1980s with that of the Grove-Barrett tandem during Barrett's tenure as CEO, it seems that the latter had significant gaps in both the clarity of their company strategy (acquisitions) and the soundness of their personnel and leadership strategy (incumbents).

## Management Style

Just prior to taking over as CEO, Craig Barrett told *Newsweek* that he had "never met anybody who's quite as direct and in-your-face as Andy [Grove]," and then added, "That's not my style." From the outset, it was clear that (as the article points out) Barrett would "be a different kind of leader from the vaunted Grove."[57]

Part and parcel of Grove's style was his practice of pushing managers to their breaking point in order to get the highest level of performance. In a recent *Fortune* article, Grove reflected on his management by stating: "The point is, there is a growth rate at which everybody fails and the whole situation results in a chaos. I feel it is my most important function (as being the highest-level manager who still has a way to judge the impending failure) to identify the maximum growth rate at which this wholesale failure phenomenon begins."[58] No doubt this practice had its trickle-down effect as managers pushed their subordinates throughout the organization, helping to institutionalize the "culture of fear" that characterized the Intel of Andy Grove. Is it then too much of a stretch to assume, based on Grove's comments above, that for Craig Barrett, being a different kind of leader would mean, in part, trying to dismantle (through his management style) the culture of fear that he inherited from Andy Grove? While he made no explicit comments to that effect, such an assumption does not seem to be unreasonable, based on his actions while CEO.

---

[57] Jennifer Tanaka, "The 'Barrett Traverse,'" *Newsweek*, 20 April 1998, 46.
[58] Richard S. Tedlow, "The Education of Andy Grove," *Fortune,* 12 December 2005, 116.

## The Discipline of Andy Grove

Understanding the ramifications of Andy Grove's and Craig Barrett's different management styles first requires an understanding of the role of discipline within Intel's culture, and any such discussion of discipline must begin with Andy Grove. According to Tim Jackson, "Andy Grove had an approach to discipline and control that made you wonder how much he had been unwittingly influenced by the totalitarian regime he had been so keen to escape."[59] There can be no mistake about it; Andy Grove was, by all accounts, an extremely disciplined individual and expected a high degree of discipline from all Intel employees. This was true whether he was demanding an important deliverable within a critical program or merely expecting a meeting to start on time, as can be seen in the following case.

In the 1970s, when the company was still relatively small, Andy Grove (then executive vice president) would favor different departments with a personal visit. On one occasion, as an employee recounts, Andy was to share some remarks and answer questions at a meeting, and arrived at the designated conference room a few minutes before it was scheduled to start. At the designated start time, Andy promptly locked the door and began the discussion. Within minutes, a few of the group's remaining employees arrived at the room but were unable to enter because the door was locked, so naturally, they knocked on the door. To their surprise and embarrassment, Andy himself opened the door and informed them that they were late and would not be able to attend the meeting—as simple as that. If, by nature, you were not quite this disciplined, experiences like this would help you to act in a disciplined fashion within the Intel environment. (On a side note, this employee also mentioned that Andy was quite polite and friendly, revealing what seems to be a soft spot for rank-and-file employees, who were generally too guileless to play politics and thereby provoke Andy's wrath.)

Without a doubt, the most notable example of Intel's culture of forced discipline was the infamous "late list," which Grove instituted in 1971 to make sure all employees arrived by 8:00 AM. The idea was vigorously opposed by most of Intel's management and its human resources department, yet Grove could not be denied, a fact that alone could cement his legacy as a tyrannical disciplinarian. He also instituted

---

[59] Tim Jackson, *Inside Intel* (New York, NY: Penguin Group, 1997), 33.

regular inspections of all Intel facilities as a means to enforce neatness throughout the company.

Being fanatical about details himself, Andy Grove expected his managers to know the intimate details of their operations, and the expectation was that results would be delivered or else Andy could publicly humiliate you. Managers would delve into and stay abreast of minute details just in order to avoid humiliation. If people were not naturally disposed to this kind of discipline, they became so under Andy, or risked facing his wrath.

Were these forced discipline tactics of Andy Grove bad, per se? They certainly gave him his desired results, but they did not imbue the culture with an enduring discipline that is borne of having self-disciplined people in the first place. Worse yet, some of the more petty measures encouraged "gaming" of the system: with the late list, for example, late-arriving employees might sit in their cars until after 9:00 AM so that they wouldn't be asked to sign the late list, because the company assumed that anyone arriving that late (after 9:00 AM) was probably a customer.[60]

The significant facet of Andy Grove's leadership was that even though discipline was forced, it still demanded focused accountability. Andy set aggressive goals, assigned accountability, and inspected managers' data for their results. When he passed the torch to Craig Barrett, the discipline dwindled: Barrett talked about discipline but rarely demanded accountability. Andy Grove had imposed discipline on the organization, but had failed to imbue it into the fabric of the company culture.

### Barrett's Rubber Band Discipline

It has been the authors' observation that under the leadership of Craig Barrett, fewer results have been delivered due to the absence of fear and forced discipline. This observation substantiates the claim that Intel does not have a culture of discipline as much as it had a stern disciplinarian (Grove) who, by the strength of his personality, was able to force the "discipline of execution" on the organization. The analogy of a rubber band could be used to illustrate what happened: discipline under Grove was like taking a rubber band, stretching it, and holding it tight to the snapping point; under Barrett, the rubber band relaxes and returns to its natural state. Since Craig Barrett didn't expect the same level of

---

[60] Ibid, 113-15.

discipline and didn't *inspect* it to the extent that Grove did, managers were able to "get by" by giving fancy presentations on how they were "challenging the status quo," when in reality they were "spinning" results while continuing to support the ineffectual status quo. In essence, it became easier to "game" or subvert the system once Craig Barrett took over as CEO.

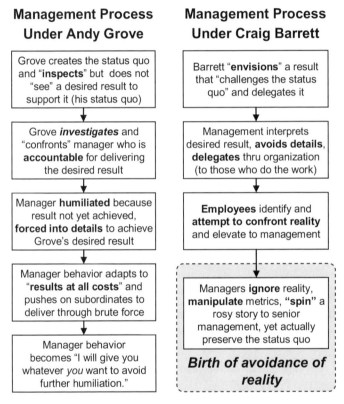

**Management Process
Under Andy Grove**

Grove creates the status quo and "**inspects**" but does not "see" a desired result to support it (his status quo)

↓

Grove *investigates* and "confronts" manager who is **accountable** for delivering the desired result

↓

Manager **humiliated** because result not yet achieved, **forced into details** to achieve Grove's desired result

↓

Manager behavior adapts to "**results at all costs**" and pushes on subordinates to deliver through brute force

↓

Manager behavior becomes "I will give you whatever *you* want to avoid further humiliation."

**Management Process
Under Craig Barrett**

Barrett "**envisions**" a result that "challenges the status quo" and delegates it

↓

Management interprets desired result, **avoids details**, **delegates** thru organization (to those who do the work)

↓

**Employees** identify and **attempt to confront reality** and elevate to management

↓

Managers **ignore** reality, **manipulate** metrics, "**spin**" a rosy story to senior management, yet actually preserve the status quo

*Birth of avoidance of reality*

When Intel's history is examined from its earliest years through the Craig Barrett era, it seems that the culture has undergone a journey through different phases of discipline and management style. The entrepreneurial, egalitarian culture of Noyce and Moore quickly gave way to the autocratic, hierarchical, forced-discipline culture of Andy Grove, which in turn paved the way for the sense of entitlement that began when Grove relinquished day-to-day operational responsibilities to Craig Barrett, and became complete when the "rubber band" was no longer being stretched.

# CULTURE

# Chapter 4

# Grove Survivors and the Birth of Entitlement

It is a curious thing in human experience, but to live through a period of stress and sorrow with another person creates a bond which nothing seems able to break.[61]

Eleanor Roosevelt

The creation of an entitled class and a culture of entitlement at Intel could not have come about without a unique set of circumstances. First, entitlement could not be possible without a source of funding. In the case of Intel, its dominance in the microprocessor market provided monopoly profits—more than enough funding to support a large entitled class. Next was the lasting effect of Grove's management style, which instilled fear in employees and engendered a survivalist mentality, a desire to hang on, cash in those stock options, and hope for better, less-stressful times—another requirement for entitlement. Those times came sooner than expected in the form of a leadership change to a more "benevolent" figure in the person of Craig Barrett—himself a survivor of the Grove-run Intel—who, from what we can surmise, appeared intent on changing the in-your-face management style that permeated the company. Finally, in order for an entitled class to be established, a class of non-entitled employees would have to be created. This class of "expendable" employees came to Intel primarily from the hordes of new hires during the 1990s.

---

[61]http://www.fabry.org/FSIG.nsf/c0fae9c0fc6a27108625666d005f3d04/7e39679ae3e7bb6b8625667a00146ce8?OpenDocument.

## The Survivor Bond

The galvanizing effect of enduring the fear-driven culture of Andy Grove cannot be overestimated and is perhaps best explained in the Eleanor Roosevelt quote at the beginning of this chapter. It's important to note that the experience of living through that climate of fear extended beyond the individual; it was an experience shared throughout the company, because in the early days of Intel, there was a Grove-driven paranoia that the company could "be put out of business the very next month."[62] The fight for daily survival was a primary concern for each employee, both individually—enduring the confrontational environment—and collectively—working together to make sure Intel did not go out of business.

The collective dynamic of this survivalist mentality can be accurately compared to that of many families who lived and fought for daily survival during the Great Depression of the 1930s. If you observe people who grew up during the Depression, you will notice that, almost without exception, they developed deep bonds with siblings and parents, which subsequently kept them extremely close for the rest of their lives (generally much closer than what is seen within today's families). The same can be said of those Intel employees who "grew up" with the company through the stressful high-growth periods and the difficult times—like 1986, when the company significantly reduced headcount through layoffs. Consistent with Eleanor Roosevelt's observation about people who suffer together, the long-time Intel employees who lived through these earlier periods of "stress and sorrow" with each other created a bond "which nothing seems able to break." *This unbreakable bond, forged in the furnace of individual and shared adversity and triumph, is the most powerful dynamic to consider when analyzing the culture and behaviors of personnel at Intel. It is a bond of familial depth.*

Paradoxically, despite passing through the fear and paranoia of the Grove grindstone, these individuals revere Andy Grove with cultish adoration, perhaps because they still yearn and are searching aimlessly for a way to recapture the glory years of Intel's past. No doubt company results and meteoric stock-price appreciation during his tenure as CEO have endeared him to the Grove Survivors. Similarly, as stated at the

---

[62] Tim Jackson, *Inside Intel* (New York, NY: Penguin Group, 1997), 142.

2005 Intel sales and marketing conference, Andy regards Intel has his "family," a term that is no doubt profound and paramount to understanding the culture of Intel.

Part and parcel of this bond among Grove Survivors is their belief that they are better than employees who are not Grove Survivors. This Grove Survivor belief is ubiquitously demonstrated throughout the culture. By virtue of having been at Intel during the boom years, these employees believe that they contributed in substantive ways to the company's success, when in reality, Intel's success can more accurately be attributed to the actions of a few competent employees and a healthy dose of serendipitous luck—the birth of the PC market and the request by IBM (International Business Machines Corp.) to use Intel's microprocessor. The Grove Survivors' belief in their substantive contributions is largely false because most any "warm body" could have performed the majority of the tasks required during this time. Yet these employees developed an inflated superiority complex (arrogance) as new employees came aboard. This characteristic of the Grove Survivors is akin to the "Self-Enhancement Bias" discovered in a study performed by Jeffrey Pfeffer at Stanford University.[63] In this study, Pfeffer compared three groups of supervisors, two of which believed that their input was not incorporated into the final product (of a project) while one group believed it was. In reality, none of the groups' input was incorporated and the final product was identical in all three cases, yet the study found that the one group of supervisors who believed their input had been substantive developed a bias: "that they had engaged in supervision led them to believe that the final product was twice as wonderful (and they were twice as wonderful), even though their actions had no actual impact!"[64] In the same way, the Grove Survivors (apart from the competent minority) who believed that their contributions to Intel during its boom years were vital to its success also believe that they are at least "twice as wonderful" as the rest of Intel's employees.

---

[63] Jeffrey Pfeffer, Robert B. Cialdini, Benjamin Hanna, and Kathleen Knopoff, "Faith in Supervision and the Self-Enhancement Bias: Two Psychological Reasons Why Managers Don't Empower Workers," *Basic and Applied Social Psychology* 20 (1998): 313-321.
[64] Jeffrey Pfeffer and Robert I. Sutton, *Hard Facts, Dangerous Half-Truths & Total Nonsense: Profiting from Evidence-Based Management* (Boston, MA: Harvard Business School Press, 2006), 198.

## Entitled and Expendable Classes of Personnel:

The lasting effect on employees who survived the fear, stress, humiliation, and brutally long hours of a fast-growing company and confrontational work environment—in short, who sacrificed so much of their being to be part of Intel, first to keep it solvent and later to reap the rewards of an ever-rising stock price—was that they made sure they would never be in a position to go through such a fearful experience again. Fear had already fueled bonds between employees who would work together to game the system in order to protect themselves and each other and survive in the workplace, and once Grove had relinquished control of operations, it is easy to see how employees—including Barrett—might have shared the following sentiment: "Hey, I've dealt with this fear enough in the past and I don't want to deal with it ever again." In essence, these employees became "entitled" when Barrett parted the sea of fear and led his fellow Grove Survivors into the "Promised Land" after they'd endured a grueling, stressful existence as part of a company that had triumphed in the marketplace under the tyrannical leadership of Andy Grove. (Interestingly, most Grove Survivors hold the benefactor of their entitlement, Craig Barrett, in derision; they blame him for the poor performance of Intel stock during his tenure as CEO and for adversely affecting their stock options and their ability to retire early.) The entitled class at Intel exists to this day and is composed primarily of Grove Survivors, as depicted in the graphic below.

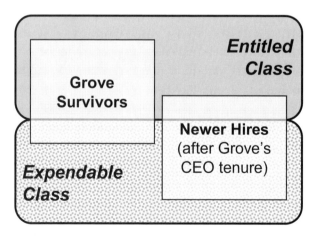

It's important to note, however, that not all Grove Survivors made it into the entitled class. Rather, the added (and more important, unwritten) distinction of being an entitled Grove Survivor came to those who were skillful enough to position company growth "beneath" them during the 1990s—that is, during the PC boom years, when Intel went from 32,600 employees (at the end of 1994) to 86,100 (by the end of 2000). As these Grove Survivors made their way into the management ranks, they developed an expectation of managerial entitlement, which became embedded in their corporate DNA.

Once the majority of Grove Survivors had made their way into the "Promised Land" of entitlement and left behind the psychological bondage of Andy Grove's Intel, they had to learn how to deal with a new type of fear. Gone were the pressures of a startup or a company fighting for survival. Gone was the confrontational work environment. A tyrannical leader no longer inspected results. No one would give you bad "360-degree feedback" (as part of the annual performance review system known as focal): your fellow Grove Survivors would say only good things about you, knowing full well that you would reciprocate. With these fears no longer present, what fear could still remain for these entitled individuals? It is the fear of being exposed as incompetent by expendable employees who outperform them.

This is a real fear, because most entitled personnel have few technical competencies. Survival during the boom years in most areas of Intel required an ability to get results—which usually came via brute force in the expediency of Intel's fast-paced environment—more than it required the technical competence needed to create repeatable business processes and sustainable results. In recent years, Intel has put a lot of effort (most of it unsuccessful) into improving business processes, partly by bringing on experienced hires, whose presence increases the risk that entitled personnel will be exposed as incompetent.

Past and current fears have become not just the glue that makes entitled Grove survivors stick together, but the gasoline fuelling a behavioral engine that keeps these individuals in the catbird seat. For members of this unofficial alliance, the overriding goal—which supersedes any corporate goals—is self-preservation and protection of an elitist way of life that allows them to reap financial fruits while delegating to expendable employees. As one entitled employee commented, "I busted my butt for years to get to this grade level and I'm going to hang on to it for as long as I can." The word "elitist" is used here to indicate both an attitude and the trickle-down method by which they avoid the fear that originally bonded them. The tool that instituted this fear under Grove, and which is used to this day, is the focal process. Now, however, focal is used to instill fear in the expendable employee ranks so that they don't challenge entitled personnel. In practice, entitled personnel are no longer subject to the focal process.

In addition to the abuse of focal to keep expendable personnel at a safe distance, entitled personnel have effectively shut the "open door policy" that allowed rank-and-file employees to speak with senior managers. True, it still exists in principle, but not in practice. There are now "channels" and hierarchical protocols that have to be followed because the entitled class, primarily composed of Grove Survivors, rules the roost.

## Entitlement and Bureaucracy

Not surprisingly, since entitled personnel lacked the ability to fix Intel's perpetually problematic business processes, many more operational personnel were hired to support the new growth focus than would have been required had those business processes remained efficient and scalable. In addition, Intel hired countless project personnel (business analysts, programmers, and others) as it attempted to fix those business processes. Finally, Intel faced the very difficult task of integrating the numerous acquisitions into the Intel way of doing business, further increasing the need for additional headcount. Though it would be reasonable to think that the acquired businesses would benefit from big-company efficiencies after coming into the Intel fold, oddly enough, this was seldom the case, as Intel's highly fragmented business processes and systems environment often required the *acquisitions* to hire additional personnel to do business "the Intel way," once they were fully integrated into the company.

As depicted in the graphic below, Intel added several layers of middle and senior management within the entitled-class bureaucracy to deal with all the growth in headcount, business volume, and business complexity resulting from the acquisitions. The growth in bureaucracy was neither a new phenomenon nor peculiar to the Craig Barrett era; rather, the excessive overhead had also existed in the Andy Grove era and was highlighted in Tim Jackson's book *Inside Intel*. What's troubling is that despite Intel's lackluster stock performance during the Craig Barrett era, it seems that management has done little or nothing to lower the high cost of its overhead, which has not remained constant, but gotten worse.

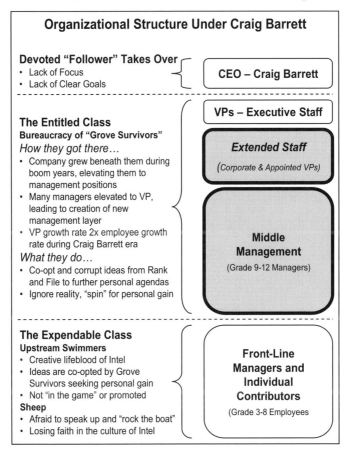

Indeed, the *entitled* bureaucracy that was ushered in and supported during the Craig Barrett era continues to reign supreme over the Intel culture under Paul Otellini's leadership. Sadly, Barrett turned a deaf ear to the *many* pleadings from rank-and-file employees to do something about this corporate cholesterol. (The chapter entitled "The Grip of Bureaucracy" will contain a more complete discussion of bureaucracy at Intel.)

## Measuring Cultural Health

An environment teeming with bureaucracy and elitist personnel cannot be healthy, despite pronouncements to the contrary from its leaders. The graphic below is intended to illuminate Barrett's comments about the health of Intel's culture relative to product performance (as quoted earlier): "product performance can't lie" proves only that Intel's culture, in *his* mind, was strong by virtue of the strong performance of Intel's products. While the outstanding performance of fab process technology development and the P6 design team products validate his words with respect to these organizations, his gauge does not apply to a growing majority of Intel, which is composed of "carpet dwellers"[65] who work in support organizations and have very remote connections, if any, to product performance.

### Measuring Intel's Cultural Health

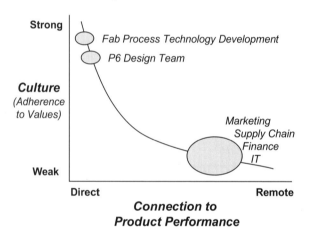

If the work of many organizations within Intel has little to do with product performance, then how can product performance be an accurate measure of the cultural health of those organizations, let alone a measure of overall corporate cultural health? It can't be, of course. Consequently, we have to look for other ways to measure cultural health of organizations whose role isn't directly connected with product performance, and this is where it gets tricky.

Intel's products must compete head-to-head in the marketplace where customers and independent analysts can compare competing products

---

[65] This somewhat derogatory term comes from fab employees and refers to Intel employees who work outside the fabs in carpeted office areas, implying that they add little real value to the company.

side-by-side to determine which is best. This is a fairly black-and-white exercise from which one can derive, albeit indirectly, some sense of the health of an organization's culture. But how do you measure the effectiveness of groups whose outputs do not provide such easy comparison with competitors? For example, how do you determine the effectiveness of something a bit fuzzier, like the implementation of information systems? At a high level, such a measure can be fairly simple if you look at something like total IT (information technology) dollars as a percentage of sales, but what about measuring the effectiveness of implementing, say, an individual application or a new business process? Did the project deliver the desired results (fully replace older systems, reduce process cycle times, improve decision making, improve productivity, improve employee morale, etc.)? Even when you can internally quantify the results, you still may not know how successful your implementation was when compared to that of your competition. Doing apples-to-apples competitive benchmarks within an industry is difficult not only in terms of gathering data, but also because competitors are reluctant to share sensitive information. You can attempt to do best-in-class benchmarking with those outside of your industry, but this can prove problematic due to those industry differences that might have a bearing on the results. The point here is that it takes digging into the details of such an implementation in order to answer the questions above and determine the implementation's effectiveness. For these reasons, the further an organization's metrics get from unambiguous product performance measures, the more difficult it is to gauge the cultural health of those organizations. Moreover, the more ambiguous the metrics for an individual or organization's outputs or results, the more susceptible they are to being subverted (gamed), as managers must usually perform detailed inspections to determine if those results were really achieved.

At Intel, where profits have been plentiful and the need to truly compete has been rare for much of its history, especially during the boom years and beyond, many, many individuals and organizations whose outputs cannot be gauged by unambiguous measures like product performance have become masters at creating and meeting *bogus* metrics in order to game the employee evaluation system. They know that management is too busy "managing upward" to dig into the details and scrutinize their results; they know they can get away with this gaming.

Such behavior clearly violates several Intel Values, obviously corrupting and weakening the culture.

This gaming is most egregious and has become an art form within support organizations that are doubly insulated from clear product-performance measures (for example, in IT groups that are in turn supporting other support organizations, like marketing, finance, supply chain planning, etc.). Those who have the detail orientation to see through the bogus metrics have a clear view of a reality that is characterized by inconsistent results, unpunished repeated mistakes, and a general lack of leadership and accountability, all of which further weaken Intel's culture. Unfortunately for Intel and its many guileless employees, Barrett and the vast majority of Intel's senior managers haven't demonstrated the detail orientation (an Intel Value) that brings the discernment needed to detect this gaming; worse yet, many of them are doing it themselves. And even if they have detected it, they have yet to demonstrate the requisite level of emotional fortitude to eradicate this behavior, because this would mean having to break their familial bonds and hold fellow Grove Survivors accountable.

As CEO, Barrett *talked* about adherence to the Intel Values, but he didn't back up his words with the same level of *inspection* that had marked the Grove era. Of course, given Intel's massive size in the Barrett era, such detailed inspections wouldn't always have been possible; nevertheless, Barrett seemed to be aloof and uncomfortable when interacting with rank-and-file employees and digging into the details of any particular problem. Contrast this with Jack Welch as CEO of GE (General Electric Co.), who not only found time, but *relished* the opportunity to dig deep into the details of a particular problem within GE in order to help find solutions and rub shoulders with rank-and-file employees.[66] Such interactions helped keep the GE culture strong, because employees saw leaders who modeled the desired behaviors. To our knowledge, no sort of deep dive ever took place while Barrett was CEO; rather, he seemed to be an elitist on top of a bureaucracy and gave greatest credence to information coming from his "direct reports"—those within his inner circle—rather than building bonds with common employees.

There remains one last stinging indictment of the sick status of Intel's

---

[66] Jack Welch, *Jack: Straight from the Gut* (New York, NY: Warner Books, 2001), 205.

culture, an indictment that is based on the words of Barrett himself. By the end of 2005, barely a year after Barrett gave his indicator for the health of the culture, Intel no longer had a technological lead, according to most industry experts who compared Intel's microprocessor products with those of its main rival, AMD. What's astonishing is that Intel lost this technological lead despite the fact that it is many times larger than AMD and has nearly infinite resources to pour into product development. Is it a stretch to suppose that the products of an ailing corporate culture rife with hierarchy, class division, bureaucracy and gaming, would under-perform those of a much smaller rival? Indeed, product performance in 2005 has betrayed Barrett's bold statement.

One could surmise that the gaming so prevalent in Intel's non-core functional areas has found its way into the realm of microprocessor design and development. As Robert Colwell points out in *The Pentium Chronicles*, marketing personnel, rather than engineers, led the NetBurst design team. Supplanting engineering from its long-standing traditional position of design program leadership, marketers demanded features, so disenfranchised engineers delivered via inelegant solutions, producing an inferior design that was prone to high power consumption and heat dissipation. Many Intel Values were broken as marketing failed to pay attention to detail, did not listen to customers, and did not allow engineering to fully participate in the process or constructively confront and solve problems. Engineering, for its part, gamed the system by forcing the results marketing had requested, knowing that marketing was more concerned with the result than with how it was achieved.

There can be little doubt that Intel's past greatness came as a result of its fab manufacturing and CPU design teams having the freedom to live the Intel Values and produce great results. But now, the desire of Grove Survivors and others to ascend into the entitled class, and the gaming associated with this desire, has spread like a cancer that is eating away at operational effectiveness, even encroaching on the strongholds of Intel's core competencies. The existence of an entitled class that does not live the Intel Values but expects the expendable class to abide by them has created conflicts in the culture that affect both classes, and an environment in which predominant behaviors for career trajectory are based on political astuteness rather than technical competence and execution.

## Evolution of Intel Culture

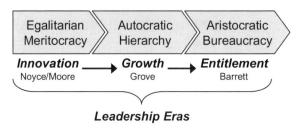

*Leadership Eras*

It's quite saddening to consider the transformation of Intel culture over the course of the leadership transition from Andy Grove to Craig Barrett. The latter wanted to be "a different kind of leader" and had the opportunity to steer the culture back toward an egalitarian meritocracy. Instead, wishing to avoid management-by-fear, he let the pendulum swing too far the other way and ushered in an era of entitlement, built a mammoth bureaucracy, and allowed gaming of the system to go unchecked—effectively killing meritocracy and damaging the company's ability to execute. Instead of restoring the health of the Intel culture by bringing behaviors in line with the published Values, Craig Barrett made things much worse.

VALUES SUMMARY

Adherence to the following Intel Values declined under the leadership of Craig Barrett:

RISK TAKING

⇒ Learn from our successes and mistakes

QUALITY

⇒ Do the right things right
⇒ Continuously learn, develop and improve

DISCIPLINE

⇒ Ensure a safe, clean and injury-free workplace
⇒ Make and meet commitments
⇒ Properly plan, fund and staff projects
⇒ Pay attention to detail

RESULTS ORIENTATION

⇒ Set challenging and competitive goals
⇒ Focus on output
⇒ Assume responsibility
⇒ Constructively confront and solve problems
⇒ Execute flawlessly

BEHAVIORS SUMMARY

The leadership actions of Craig Barrett exacerbated the following behaviors:

⇒ Co-opting
⇒ Preserving the status quo
⇒ Managing upward
⇒ Ignoring realities
⇒ Avoiding details
⇒ Lack of punishment for egregious repeated failures

# Chapter 5

# Dysfunctional Differentiation

Every company has created a perfect reward system to generate the precise behavior they are currently getting.[67]

Eli Goldratt

Any time you pit a good performer against a bad system, the system will win every time.[68]

Geary Rummler and Alan Brache

The notion that Andy Grove built an incredibly strong management team before handing over the CEO reins to his chosen successor, Craig Barrett, is still prevalent. Indeed, some would contend that there is an aura surrounding "Intel managers" because they are so highly capable, demanding, and fearless, essentially made in the image of Andy Grove. However, if you examine the actions of Barrett and Intel management in general, you will see that since Grove's departure as CEO, Intel managers have acted as if they were lost. As the company moved into uncharted waters with the acquisition strategy, Intel managers seemed more comfortable retreating to a "safety in numbers" approach to their work—huddling around the microprocessor business model for everything they did.

Such behavior belies the image of daring and toughness built up under the tutelage of Andy Grove. How could this be? Perhaps the simple answer is that most Intel managers lacked technical competence and therefore acted with great caution so as not to risk losing their entitled positions. In the autocratic hierarchy of Grove's Intel, technical know-

---

[67] Quote of the day, www.excite.com.
[68] BPM Conference, San Francisco, November 2004.

how was not essential for the majority of managers who worked outside the company's areas of core competency. To succeed in their jobs, they merely had to carry out Andy's orders, provided Intel remained highly profitable from the work being done by the few technically-competent personnel in the key fab manufacturing and microprocessor design organizations. Under this arrangement, Intel never felt the need to develop robust methods for differentiating its diverse sets of employees and assessing them based on technical competence.

However, since Grove's tenure, it has become apparent that individuals who lack the critical attribute of technical competence have difficulty leading their organizational sectors to outstanding levels of performance. When you look beyond the veil of microprocessor profits, it becomes apparent that the leaders of non-microprocessor groups have been unable to focus money and resources in directions that would lead to profitable operations. The best example of this problem has been the money-losing operations of the now-defunct Intel Communications Group (ICG). The lack of effective employee differentiation with respect to technical competence has been a key cultural flaw enabling the establishment and growth of Intel's bureaucracy, and to this day it prevents the company from filling its management pipeline with promising future leaders.

In this chapter we will discuss (1) how Intel hired personnel at different points in its history, (2) how Intel differentiates employees to place them in different positions, and (3) how lack of technical competence led to decision-by-committee and the growth of bureaucracy. Along the way we will contrast Intel's approaches with those of General Electric, arguably the industry benchmark for differentiating employees, developing leaders, and fighting bureaucracy.

## Getting In the Door at Intel

Robert Noyce and Gordon Moore. These two names alone did more than anything else to attract highly talented engineers to their fledgling startup back in 1968. "It was their charisma, their leadership, their contacts, and their reputation that brought together a group of the most talented engineers in the world and established the framework that allowed scientific creativity to flow."[69] So promising were the opportunities at Intel—not just in terms of the development and selling of products, but also in terms of working in an egalitarian environment— that new hires were willing to take pay cuts and lesser roles within the company, just to get "in the door." The best and brightest as well as proven industry experts flocked to Intel in the early days and were instrumental in achieving the product and process breakthroughs that were foundational to the company's success for decades to come.

As the company grew throughout its first decade, it experienced a change in philosophy regarding its approach to recruiting. In 1973, within five years of the company's founding, Andy Grove reportedly said that "we don't hire anyone [professional staffers] under twenty-five."[70] But by 1978, after Intel had been in existence long enough to develop its distinct company culture, its philosophy shifted and the majority of new hires were "NCGs" (new college graduates), on the assumption that it would be easier to train NCGs in "the Intel way" of doing things than it would be to retrain experienced hires. Intel's reputation as an exciting growth company made it possible for Intel to choose from among the very best students to fill the never-ending demand for new hires. Indeed, Intel has been a growth company for most of its existence, and getting enough people has played a large part in supporting this growth.

Hiring smart NCGs did not necessarily mean Intel would have the right people to challenge the status quo. On the contrary, these new hires were trained to merely suggest changes within the context of the existing system: most did not possess the wisdom that comes from having significant previous work experience before joining Intel. They might have thought they were being good Intel citizens and challenging the status quo, but in reality they were merely "shuffling the cards within the same deck," rather than introducing an entirely new deck of cards. So instead of perpetuating the Intel Value of challenging the status quo, the change in philosophy from hiring experience to hiring NCGs who could be molded to Intel's own image was a key factor driving Intel's legendary arrogance and, for the next 20 years, the "not invented here" syndrome. This change was pivotal because it led to "corporate tunnel

---

[69] Tim Jackson, *Inside Intel* (New York, NY: Penguin Group, 1997), 7.
[70] Ibid, 51.

vision" in which experience and "fresh eyes" were virtually non-existent in the culture, and created an environment where people would look inward for BKMs[71] rather than outside of Intel. In more recent years, a pattern has emerged, which sees experienced, "world beater" hires getting frustrated with their inability to challenge the status quo and eventually leaving the company.

It's important to note our reference above to Intel's getting "*enough* people" but not "enough of *the right* people" to support its growth. This detail is critical to understanding Intel's management of personnel. By the mid 1970s, Intel's main product innovations had already taken place and the culture and continuous improvement processes for (1) product design and (2) fab manufacturing had been established. Intel's fortunes would rest on these two core competencies, where it was among the best, if not the best, in the industry. But because of this strength, getting "the *right* people" into the right jobs outside of these competencies was never a priority, and in order to stay true to its slogan, "Intel Delivers," ancillary tasks like purchasing, distribution, and customer fulfillment and support were executed via highly fragmented, forced, manual, and ad hoc business processes. Personnel in these areas were given very narrow responsibilities so that the risk of process failure would be reduced, and more emphasis was placed on having *enough* people rather than *the right* people, because it was known that Intel's high-volume, high-margin business could compensate for the resulting gross inefficiencies elsewhere in the company. To Intel's credit, it has been amazingly effective at delivering product over the years, but much of this success has ridden on the backs of untold armies of "worker bees" who have been stuck in unsophisticated, menial, and unfulfilling jobs, and who have stayed in their positions only because they didn't have the skills to go elsewhere or because the perpetually rising stock price appeased their ambitions to look outside for better opportunities. Since high growth has dominated much of Intel's history, retaining employees became paramount to supporting that growth; indeed, against the backdrop of a constantly growing company, the fear of losing personnel can deeply affect the psyche of a company. While not discussed openly, the result at Intel is a prevailing attitude that, especially as it pertains to higher-level managers, the company must do all in its power to retain those

---

[71] Best Known Methods

individuals, even in those ancillary areas where management's technical and leadership skills are unconscionably low by industry standards. While it's true that Intel has passed through a few difficult periods that required some layoffs, these have not been of a sufficient magnitude or duration to reverse this ingrained fear of losing personnel. Nor has the existence of highly fragmented and inefficient business processes been enough to motivate meaningful personnel changes in poorly performing functional areas. Why? Because historically, these inefficient and barely workable business processes have adequately supported the overall business objective of delivering product. And compared with the rest of industry, Intel has maintained an astonishing level of profitability due to its dominant market position in microprocessors.

Now that times are changing for Intel—we're seeing the decreasing relevance of Moore's Law in the eyes of consumers, more competition from AMD across all of Intel's CPU markets (server, desktop, and mobile), continued lack of profit outside of microprocessors, increasing customer impatience with Intel's lack of customer orientation in product design and supply chain agility—it's becoming clearer that the company should commit to a robust approach to recruiting, developing, and managing personnel. Moreover, even if the company can regain the technological lead over AMD and stave off the commoditization of microprocessor products, there are significant efficiencies and incremental profits to be gained by addressing the excessive overhead and inefficiency issues that have led to Intel's gargantuan, wasteful bureaucracy. In plain language, the company needs to cut the fat at the top and in the middle in order to become operationally lean and further improve profits.

## Results at All Costs

One of the more common behaviors of managers is to delegate an action required (AR) when it's received from above. The most common statement managers make to their employees is: "I don't care how it gets done, so long as it gets done." This is a remnant from the early days of microprocessor growth rates, when demand for product far exceeded Intel's ability to meet it, and Andy Grove established a pattern of urgency for everything. The actions of Andy and his managers during these high growth years created short-term, quick-fix behaviors and gestalt that settled into the culture. As the company and headcount grew, this "results at all costs" [72] behavior became the default reaction of practically all managers and their corresponding employees. Unfortunately, this type of behavior doesn't create the right kind of environment for sustainable business processes over the long term, but rather serves as more of a Band-Aid for the moment. This pattern of "results at all costs" also describes the management "gaming" at Intel, the process for impressing your managers. Some rank-and-file employees joke about "grab the glory and run" practices whereby project managers quickly get as far away as possible from the results they have just achieved in order to distance themselves from the inevitable reality that those results will not be sustainable.

One Intel employee who spent several years working at Toyota contrasted the two companies by saying Intel has a *results* orientation whereas Toyota has a *process* orientation. Instead of placing explicit focus on achieving results, Toyota's "kaizen" culture lets the desired results flow as a natural byproduct of its repeatable and continuously improving business processes. This stands in stark contrast to the Intel orientation in areas outside of fab manufacturing.

Other insider comments corroborate this observation. A different employee has noted how often Intel works with certain customers to do extensive tweaking of Intel products in order to get their performance on a par with similar out-of-the-box products from the competition. Even a minimally observant person within the Intel environment can find countless cases showing that Intel's imbalanced "results orientation" has led to gross inefficiencies in business processes, not to mention political gaming for personal gain—getting an "outstanding" on your focal performance review. People expend a lot of energy to create the perception of getting quick results, and when this is combined with management's short attention span and lack of detail orientation or discernment, the results are noted and forgotten before anyone is wiser to the eventual outcome.

Of course, corporations are in business to produce goods and services (results) for which others will be willing to pay (results again). When

---

[72] "Results at all costs" (as defined by the authors) is a management paradigm unique to Intel, which tells employees to get the results by any method necessary; managers don't care "how," just that the result is achieved.

you are a fast-growing company, as Intel was for much of its history, a results orientation can be good, even if many of the results are produced by applying an inordinate amount of "human glue." You can't fault Intel for its results orientation of the past (under Grove) or ignore how certain results—even if achieved by brute force—supported its stellar financial performance. However, sustained performance in an organization is more likely to be achieved when there is a balance between *what* the results are and *how* they are consistently achieved. This has been proven and documented in many other companies, most notably GE; however, what separates companies is acknowledging processes and orienting management practices to them in order to sustain operational performance over time. Intel has excelled with this primarily in fab manufacturing and product design.

It is no accident that one of Intel's biggest competitive advantages is found in fab process technology development, where a *process orientation* reigns supreme. One could easily argue that the sustainable results flowing naturally from this *process* orientation fuel Intel's profitability and, unfortunately, subsidize the *results* orientation and gaming that take place throughout the rest of Intel. This dynamic duality is at the core of Intel's complex culture, where an extremely successful process orientation leads to remarkable financial results, while the pursuit of results-by-brute-force fuels the rise through the ranks of politically gaming personnel.

When you look at other functional areas within Intel, it is obvious that a process orientation is sorely lacking. The "results at all costs" culture so deeply ingrained within many Intel managers ignores the *how* you achieve results to such a degree that managers shrink from making the really tough decisions needed to improve processes, knowing that changes for the better may negatively hit the immediate results. In other words, managers sacrifice long-term sustainability for short-term results, and sacrifice the good of the company for their personal gain. This is one of the predominant behaviors of the entitled class, who are so preoccupied with advancing their own careers that they position themselves annually for the focal performance reviews instead of doing the right things for the company. This phenomenon has so clouded decision making at Intel that more bad decisions (having negative operational consequences) are made than good ones, at least outside the core areas of the company. Another troubling ramification of this imbalanced focus on results is the practice of suppressing the upward flow of bad news. Unfortunately, these problems never seem to make it to the forefront of senior management's consciousness.

## Contrasting Employee Differentiation at GE and Intel

If you were to compare General Electric's method for differentiating employees and cultivating leaders with Intel's, you would see that they are as diametrically opposed as night is to day. When Jack Welch took over as CEO of General Electric, he realized that cultivating the right people was the most important factor in making GE a great company. It was about finding competent individuals and nurturing them to become great leaders who would, in turn, instill in others consistently great performance. When Welch introduced this idea to his senior executives, it was met with blank stares—no one really got it. It took at least two years to catch on and it meant that Welch had to make some hard choices about how he was going to institute his ideas within the GE culture. That he obviously prevailed over the next twenty years was one of the great legacies of Jack Welch's tenure as head of GE. He instituted a formalized, systematic process for differentiating people. Differentiation was more than just getting results, although results were a large part of that differentiation: another significant element of it was ensuring that individuals had the intellectual capacity to come up with new ideas that challenged old assumptions, and the integrity to get their team to achieve results through means that were completely consistent with the published company Values.

At GE, the main vehicle for testing and showcasing an individual's technical competence and leadership potential is a process-focused industry methodology for operational improvement called Six Sigma. The philosophy, principles, and practices of Six Sigma emphasize individual attention to detail and a problem-solving methodology that is embedded not only in GE's management development program, but also within the DNA of its corporate culture. All employees must make their way through Six Sigma training, progressing to Green and Black Belt "assignments." The successful completion of these assignments becomes a rite of passage to advancement and leadership positions, provided that the results achieved are sustainable and other "soft" skills are met, so that employees don't "kiss up and kick down" to achieve those results. As employees continue their Six Sigma assignments, the scope of such assignments keeps getting broader, thereby testing each person's leadership potential. To succeed in one of these assignments also requires the ability to solve complex problems, and can only be achieved when team members and leaders possess an adequate level of technical competence, including a thorough knowledge of the details within the business unit. Using this process, GE is able to develop a corps of technically competent, detail-oriented leaders who live and exemplify company values and achieve lasting results. All senior management personnel appointed at GE, including CEO Jeff Immelt, have at one time or another had a Six Sigma Black Belt assignment.

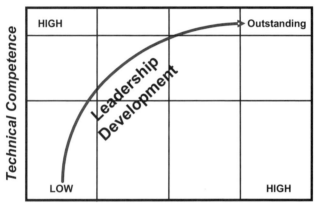

**Ability to Implement Change & Get Results**

## The GE Benchmark

Contrast GE's methodical approach with Intel's mantra of "results at all costs," the vestige of its entrepreneurial startup days when, if things were not done fast, then the company might go out of business. Those individuals who could achieve results quickly were the ones who were recognized as performers and subsequently promoted. Intel developed a "speed over quality" culture where systemic fixes to problems were ignored for Band-Aid solutions, and where little emphasis was placed on how people got results because no one had time to reflect, due to the hectic pace and growth of the company. Thus, "results at all costs" became embedded in the culture of entrepreneurship and still exists today in the Grove Survivors, with the consequence that lower-level personnel tended to be expendable, and there's no "soft side" to how people are evaluated and measured at Intel. This lack of rigor in identifying potential leaders becomes dangerous when you consider that Intel employees are told, "your career is literally your business."[73] Not that there is anything wrong with owning your career, but when this approach is left unchecked—without the oversight of discerning, detail-oriented managers—the environment becomes "gamed" or subverted and the "cream" does not rise to the top. People become obsessed with self-advancement and turn into sycophants who focus exclusively on positioning themselves and "managing upward"—setting themselves up for promotion by creating the perception that they are getting things done.

Intel's main vehicle for differentiating employees is the annual performance management system called "focal" that is based on "360-degree" performance feedback from an employee's peers, subordinates, and managers. It is intended to be a merit-based system designed to reward individuals who get results and perform according to Intel Values. However, there are two fundamental problems with the focal process at Intel. First is that the 360 performance system can be gamed because it is based on peer input. It's obvious to any Intel employee how to game the system: submit a short list of names of people you know who like you. One Intel employee summed up his focal appropriately by saying, "This year I think my focal will be 'popular with no results,' so I should be OK."[74] Many companies eventually realize this system does not work in the long run. GE, which has been in business for over 100 years, discovered this fact by trial and error. In his autobiography *Jack: Straight from the Gut*, Jack Welch stated:

> Finding a way to differentiate people across a large company has been one of the hardest things to do...We led the charge into "360-degree evaluations," which take into account the views of peers and subordinates.
> We loved the idea—for the first few years it helped us locate the "horses' asses" who "kissed up and kicked down." Like anything driven by peer input, the system is capable of being "gamed" over the long haul. People began saying nice things about one another so they would come out with good ratings.

---

[73] Andrew S. Grove, *Only the Paranoid Survive* (New York, NY: Doubleday, 1996) 6.
[74] Employee wished to remain anonymous.

The "360s" are now only used in special situations.[75]

As we have seen, Intel's fixation with getting results at all costs has created a corporate gestalt that's addicted to the quick fix. During the entrepreneurial days, it worked because of Intel's smaller size and the immediacy with which things could get done. However, now that Intel is a larger, more mature company with the corresponding systemic problems derived from high growth, this quick-fix gestalt no longer works. The Grove Survivors retain this mantra in their DNA, but it translates into unrealistic expectations for those on the receiving end of delegation. The unrealistic expectations are one of the key drivers that erode risk taking and, more importantly, innovation. Innovation requires deep meditation and pondering, neither of which is appreciated or rewarded because of the unrealistic time constraints put on individuals. A results orientation forces managers and employees to become fixated with hitting indicators or targets, even if their hits don't produce sustainable results. In many cases, managers and employees feel they will lose their jobs if they don't deliver the assigned targets, and this can result in "brute force" methods or, worse, an erosion of ethical behavior, which inclines individuals to fudge their results or devise indicators that make them look good in the eyes of their manager.

The second fundamental problem with focal is that the process does not differentiate the degree of technical competence required to perform in a job. Your competence is supposed to be implicit in the results you are claiming. For example, if you are working in the supply chain domain, what are the criteria for entry, and what are the criteria for maintaining a high degree of competence and performance? Obviously there would be a knowledge component (e.g. a degree in an operations-related field) plus an experience component with additional criteria for maintaining that competency over time (e.g. Association for Professional Operations Management—APICS—certification). However, the ability to dive deeply within a specific domain, understand it, and apply it, is missing from Intel's criteria for measuring value. The authors have time and again talked with people informally during our years at Intel, and nearly every employee has made comments like "my manager has no background in areas pertinent to my job duties," "I know more than my

---

[75] Jack Welch, *Jack: Straight from the Gut* (New York, NY: Warner Books, 2001), 157.

manager," "I have to tell my manager what direction we should be taking." This is obviously a common occurrence at many companies and therefore is not unique to Intel; however, what's notable is the degree to which it's prevalent outside of the core areas of the company.

There is no compulsory directive to continuously improve knowledge in specific domains. People trust that *you* know the details of your business because they don't know or *don't want* to know those details, and so during focal, it is assumed that the results claimed are true; their veracity isn't questioned ("If it sounds good, it must be good"; "she's been at Intel 20 years, so I'm not going to dive into the details to find out if she's lying"). The very notion that many years spent working at Intel automatically provide one with enough knowledge and experience for promotion is ludicrous, but it holds much credence with the "ruling elite" in these other domains. More telling is how many people over the years claim ownership of the same achievements for highly visible programs on their monthly reports, as part of their focal. Conversely, if the true owner of the achievement is not a vocal, self-promoting employee, then he or she runs the risk of not getting any credit for the achievement. Gaming has reached such virulent levels that behaviors don't support reality and words don't reflect it.

If you operate in an environment where managers have an aversion to the details because they did not "grow up" with the rigor of anything like GE's Six Sigma assignments, then it becomes very easy to feign results in order to support your counterfeit competence. In such environments, the "results at all costs" mantra facilitates false perceptions of employee technical competence and ultimately leads to inaccurate differentiation of personnel. The individuals who are best at gaming the system or most politically astute are the ones who get promoted. This is the Peter Principle at its finest.

When promotions and leadership opportunities arise in the "you own your career" world of Intel, people with high technical skills who generate tangible results are routinely overlooked in favor of the upward-managing "show horses" (or, as Jack Welch put it, the "horses asses"), who tend to be sycophantic, present specious plans that are rarely implemented (and when they are it's via brute force), and claim achievements that are not scrutinized by undiscerning managers. Consequently, the right people are not getting into the critical positions to lead Intel in the many areas where change is sorely needed: rather, many of the wrong people repeatedly land in key positions. It's an "old boy network" where people have been in the same jobs too long, have taken Intel's monopoly profits and their jobs for granted, and don't have the "fresh eyes" to successfully address the company's current set of challenges.

Another contrast between GE and Intel is in the area of mentoring. At GE, business leaders are given responsibility to mentor promising (differentiated) individuals in order to build the company's leadership pipeline. A key part of leaders' accountability, one that's baked into their evaluations, is whether or not their mentee gets promoted. GE tracks this metric at a corporate level. At Intel, being a mentor is merely an informal, extracurricular activity that neither helps nor hurts in your annual evaluation. A person wanting to find a mentor must expend great effort because it's difficult to find a more senior manager who (1) is willing to devote the time to you and (2) possesses deep, detailed technical competence in your given domain. All a senior manager at Intel can do is give you insight into how to "influence" and "build your network" (read: improve your popularity) or become the "career crane" that can pull you upward in grade levels.

So, how is leadership cultivated at Intel when there are no formal accountability and reward systems for identifying and channeling the right candidates into a leadership pipeline? The answer is simple: it isn't. Frankly, many of the employees who "grew up" at Intel have been riding in the "gravy train" cars of the Moore's Law Express for such a long time that they have lost the ability (assuming they had it in the first place) to distinguish the important differences among personnel. This *inattention* to detail is just one example of how behaviors at Intel differ from the company's published Values ("Pay attention to detail"). It's odd to think that such a notable engineering company wouldn't put more effort and *science* into differentiating employees in order to identify and develop leaders, and to realize even more value from existing knowledge capital.

## Unwritten Methods for Differentiating Employees

Intel's lack of a systematic, detail-oriented method of differentiating talent, coupled with its rapid growth and failure to reinvigorate it has led to the incubation of certain underlying behaviors that we will describe in the following paragraphs, providing an etiology of the creation and growth of bureaucracy at Intel.

During the high growth years, there was a free-for-all just to get warm bodies to operate the barely workable business processes and help sustain the rapid growth of the company. The focal process was really the only mechanism for ensuring that performance and results were rewarded, without regard to whether or not the selected people were capable of the responsibilities given them upon promotion. Over time, other unspoken criteria emerged that would guide management to choose who would be inserted into the leadership pipeline. These criteria were: years of service or tenure, grade level, one's "network" (popularity), and one's willingness to receive direction and delegated orders without push-back (i.e., servility). These criteria became far more important measures of value in the Intel culture than technical competence. This was especially true in areas where job or group performance metrics are ambiguous or subject to "spinning" and manipulation—generally in those functional areas farthest from manufacturing, where product performance provides clear metrics that cannot lie. These measures of perceived employee value may sound like gross oversimplifications, but they are manifest in countless ways on a daily basis within the company.

### Years of Service

Years of service—*specifically at Intel*—is *always* the first piece of information shared by employees as they introduce themselves to a new team or group of other employees. It doesn't matter whether you're fresh out of college or a seasoned industry veteran with an impressive, multi-year corporate track record prior to your pre-Intel career. What *does* matter is whether you are a Grove Survivor. This piece of information is the fastest and most reliable way for long-time employees to determine your "worth" (in their eyes) to the company—in much the same way that dogs inform themselves by sniffing each other's behinds. Furthermore, the prevailing belief at Intel is "we're different," and while periodic lip service is given to the importance of understanding industry BKMs, the reality is that outside knowledge and experience are generally not valued within Intel.

At this point, you may be asking why the Grove Survivor bond, developed prior to 1998, is still so important many years later. What you still have at Intel is a sizeable group of long-time employees who grew up, bonded, and survived together under Andy Grove's leadership. And make no mistake about it, being a "Grove Survivor" carries with it an unspoken "rite of passage" to credibility, *perceived* competence, prominence, and leadership opportunities within the company.

To be clear, favoritism among Grove Survivors is really a form of nepotism as these individuals share a familial bond. One senior Intel human resources manager[76] recently acknowledged that much of Intel is plagued with manager-subordinate and peer-to-peer relationships that have been in place 20 years or more, but he also lamented that the company seems lost or unwilling to take bold actions to shake things up, to break these incestuous bonds. When new employees come into a group or team where such decades-long relationships exist, they have no chance of breaking into this "club," no matter how competent they are, no matter how sincere and pure their motives, no matter how much they live and practice relationship-building skills and principles from the likes of Dale Carnegie and Steven Covey, no matter how much they exemplify the Intel Values. Inevitably, new employees will be victims of discrimination—not in the traditional sense of discrimination based on gender, race, religion, or sexual orientation—but an *implicit*, and at times, *overt* discrimination that occurs because they have not been at Intel long enough…they aren't Grove Survivors. Indeed, for better or for worse, years of service at Intel is the chief criterion for differentiating Intel employees, period.

### Grade Level

A thorough understanding of the Intel merit system is warranted before we proceed. Intel uses a job-code-based "grade" system for classifying and compensating employees. To put it simply, the higher the grade level, the more important the title you carry, along with compensation. Employees are also classified as "exempt" (salaried) and "non-exempt" (paid hourly), but for purposes of this discussion, only the "exempt" grade levels will be examined, as those are the ones most relevant to this book. Exempt employee levels go from grade 3 up to grade 15+, where a grade 3 is typically a college graduate or a non-

---

[76] Employee wishes to remain anonymous.

exempt employee with a number of years' experience who becomes a salaried employee. Newly minted recruits with master's degrees (MBAs) typically come in between grade 5 and grade 7, depending on what university they attended. Ivy League MBAs who choose to come to Intel will come in as grade 7 or 8, whereas second- and third-tier MBAs usually start lower.

Grades 3 through 8 are considered the "rank-and-file" professional employees of Intel. These people are closest to the operational details and work where the "rubber meets the road" on a daily basis. Grade 6 and grade 7 are considered front-line managers. Grades 8 and 9 are considered middle managers and grades 10 and above are considered senior managers.

As employees approach grades 8 and 9, their time is supposedly divided 50/50 between strategic and tactical activities. In practice, employees at these grades tend to think they have paid their dues, so the real percentage tends to be 20% tactical and 80% strategic, where "strategic" time is spent delegating or putting together PowerPoint presentations for the next-level manager. What's noteworthy is that the criteria for grade levels are inconsistent across Intel. For example, a grade 8 in a purchasing organization often has incredible responsibility, the scope of which may involve managing anywhere from four to twelve direct reports, dealing with CEOs of suppliers, and having spending authority that can run into the hundreds of millions. But in the information technology group, a grade 8 business analyst may be primarily responsible for gathering requirements for applications solutions, and have no direct reports or contact with customers, suppliers, or senior managers within Intel.

If you look at the growth of Intel over the last 15 years, those individuals who in 1990 ranked at about grade 6 benefited the most from corporate growth by the time 2000 rolled in. The organizations of which they were a part grew underneath them, and by virtue of their years of service they received grade-level promotions and were assigned to manage personnel that were accumulating in their respective areas. There are, of course, extreme examples of people who started out as secretaries or line technicians and went on to grade 12, leading whole divisions. A lot of these people are still there today, doing the job exactly the same way they did it 20 years ago, neither changing with the times nor improving their level of technical competence.

The grade level system creates the perception of competence: the higher a person's grade level, the greater the perceived competence of that person. Thus, grade level represents another important measure of perceived value for Intel employees and usually is strongly correlated to years of service at Intel. This is not surprising, given the fact that Intel has a strong "promote from within" philosophy. During the high-growth 1990s, the average annual headcount growth (see chart below[77]) was at its peak, and the long-time employees were the logical choices to be elevated to their respective grade levels in order to manage the incoming "newbies." When you marry the "promote from within" philosophy to the phenomenal headcount growth, it's easy to see that the "Grove Survivors" were in the best positions to secure increasingly available management positions and higher grade levels in the late 1990s.

### Intel Headcount Growth, 1995-2000

| Year | Total Headcount | Headcount Growth | Headcount Growth Rate |
|------|-----------------|------------------|-----------------------|
| 2000 | 86,100 | 15,900 | 23% |
| 1999 | 70,200 | 5,700 | 9% |
| 1998 | 64,500 | 800 | 1% |
| 1997 | 63,700 | 15,200 | 31% |
| 1996 | 48,500 | 6,900 | 17% |
| 1995 | 41,600 | 9,000 | 28% |
| 1994 | 32,600 | n/a | n/a |

From 1995 through 2000 headcount grew over 18% per year. Most of this growth occurred "below" existing personnel who were elevated into higher grade levels in the management ranks.

Generally speaking, expendable personnel are the ones who uncover the problems and elevate them to management. One of Intel's original, unwritten values says that the person closest to a problem should take the lead or ownership in fixing the problem. This value was instituted by Robert Noyce when he founded Intel, and it applied to things as simple as a piece of paper on the hallway floor—if you found it, you took responsibility for picking it up and properly disposing of it—and as complex as a defect in the manufacturing line—if you identified it, you

---

[77] Annual Reports, Intel Corporation, 1997 through 2004.

became accountable for fixing it. Now, however, the culture's unspoken rule dictates that only someone who has been at Intel for a while should take charge of fixing the problem because they have the "history and experience" required to do it successfully in the Intel environment.

High-grade-level managers even seek out problems that will give them visibility, a situation that promotes an ongoing game of "musical chairs" among program managers, especially in the IT and supply chain areas. This has bred a culture of mistrust among the rank and file because the higher-grade-level personnel co-opt programs away from the people who have the knowledge to run them. When these high-profile programs don't deliver the results within the timeframe to which they were originally committed, the program leaders are not held accountable and merely "switch chairs" before the music is over. As one worker-bee employee put it, these leaders "grab the glory and run" before the full magnitude of the program failure is apparent. The act of grabbing the glory amounts to securing the funding for programs and getting rewarded for the *projected* (unrealized) benefits, and then escaping accountability when the program fails. The amount of effort that goes into positioning to get program funding and convincing management of potential success supports the gaming of the system by higher-grade people, who receive accolades and ultimately, further promotions.

In short, the prevailing mentality at Intel is, if you've been around long enough, you know Intel well enough to be successful in getting things done and achieving results. This is why Intel chooses to appoint Intel "lifers" to lead important programs instead of technically competent rank-and-file personnel who identify problems in the first place and are best suited to fix them systemically. Programs are managed by someone who doesn't understand—and *doesn't want* to understand—the details of the problem, how to fix the problem, the difficulties in fixing the problem, how long it will take, and finally, lacks the right resources to do the difficult work. The consequences of this practice include programs that are grossly overstaffed, that never deliver on time, that deliver poor-quality solutions (if they can deliver at all), and whose leaders are not held accountable when things go wrong.

## Building Your Network

The practice of building a "network" within Intel is really a function of your years of service, the amount of job-hopping you have done within the company, and whether you are perceived as a person who gets results. It is very much about mounting your own personal marketing campaign, which indicates how adept you are at being a popular politician. While many individuals recognize the existence of this behavior, it is condoned because Intel employees are told, "you own your career"—a statement that can be viewed as an indirect admission by Intel that it is not doing the difficult work of systematically differentiating and mentoring employees to fill its leadership pipeline.

Your network is composed of people who *like* you and who have been around roughly as long as you have. As pointed out earlier in the chapter, you and others in your network have shared many experiences, so you feel a bond that in most cases is like blood. You develop work dependencies on these people, especially when projects or initiatives have overlapping deliverables. Many people in your network are part of your support base, much like voters in a politician's constituency. Your network becomes particularly useful when the year-end performance review process begins. Many people in your network will be positive contributors to your 360. This network ensures a constant stream of positive performance feedback based upon that blood-bond created from the shared experiences of growing up at Intel.

The phenomenon of building a network is not unique to Intel. What is unique is the importance placed on that network when it comes to important program decisions and differentiating people for promotions and leadership assignments. Sadly, popularity supersedes competence to perform in the job. Individuals who get promoted to positions they are not qualified for end up delegating to someone who they believe *is* capable of doing the work required, while they co-opt a healthy portion of the credit, promoting themselves as the ones responsible for identifying the opportunity and achieving the results, thus securing their role as a "go-to" person for a more senior manager.

### Servility

Along with years of service, grade level, and network, there's one more method of differentiating employees at Intel. It's an employee's willingness to take orders and direction without "pushing back," and especially without questioning or challenging the manager's strategy or direction. In other words, the network of long-time employees and delegator-managers look favorably upon a person's servility.

The practice of being servile is much more complicated than it may seem at first glance. It's more than merely displaying fawning, sycophantic behavior. The employee must be skilled at "smart talk" in order to give the impression that he or she is tough, independent-minded, and willing to challenge the status quo (an Intel Value); yet for political reasons, toughness or push-back must never be directed upward, and rarely laterally; it is mostly directed downward. However, this is not the classic "kiss up and kick down" management model either, because tough talk is used to manipulate directional decisions that attack peripheral status quo practices, but do not attack the root causes, which would truly overturn the management apple cart. Consequently, the fawning behavior directed toward managers is all the more powerful and difficult to discern, because those who display it appear to be very tough and critical in the majority of their interactions (downward), and thus increase the value of the deferential "respect" which they direct upward. Yes, it takes a special breed of person to skillfully create the perception of being a leader, even as one fulfills the desires of one's superiors to maintain the status quo.

The authors believe this behavior came from Andy Grove's management style. When underlings would make suggestions about how to improve things, Andy's first response would be to reject the ideas, even when they turned out to be good for the company (remember the Will Kauffman example earlier). However, sooner or later Andy would give in, once data were presented and the argument for changing direction was supported by that data. One had to appeal to Andy's logic by having data, but had also to be prepared for a browbeating just because it was Andy. The significance of Andy's behavior is that employees learned more from observing and emulating it than from any of his verbal feedback or insight.

This phenomenon of modeling the observed behavior of leaders rather than listening to what they said or adhering to the published Values led to the behavioral inflection point that set the stage for the Grove Survivors, who felt entitled to behave the way Andy did, though they didn't possess the corresponding discipline of execution or intellectual honesty. Once a person reaches a certain level in management, the prevailing attitude is, "I can rebuff you" (like Andy), "but you can't rebuff me" (because I survived the Grove era and now I'm entitled by grade level, years of service, etc.). This, of course, is the antithesis of the published Intel Values but reflects the unspoken Intel culture. The predominant management behavior is to delegate orders to subordinates so that they follow them blindly. Often individuals will realize that the direction either does not make sense or is not the right approach for the company. The newer a person is to Intel, the more likely they are to challenge the manager's direction, only to be rebuffed or, worse, put on a corrective action plan because the manager views the challenge to his or her authority as a performance problem.

Unlike the situation with Andy Grove, who would entertain challenges if they were detailed and data-driven, most current Intel managers will not engage in a dialogue because they are now part of the entitled class, and possibly they are afraid of being exposed as incompetent—especially when presented with data that challenge their direction. Managers even resort to bullying their subordinates, using the focal process to punish them by giving them a rating of "below expectations" or worse, "improvement required." There are many ways this can happen.

First, the employee is targeted for having questioned direction (or for no other reason than classic bullying), but it is done in such a way as to avoid any appearance of illegal discrimination. Managers will then study the strengths and weaknesses of the employee and, through micromanagement tactics, destroy the employee's position by withholding training or direction, or pressuring the employee to do something that is not consistent with what he or she knows is the right approach. If the employee asks for training, the manager will deny that training on the grounds of expense or schedule requirements. If he asks for direction, the manager gives him verbal misdirection and later denies that it ever occurred. The objective is to cause as much stress as possible for targeted employees: give them unrealistic tasks with impossible schedules; emphasize their weaknesses; fault their work on a continuous basis; and lie about what occurs in verbal one-on-one meetings. In the weekly report, take credit for the good things that the targeted employee has done during the week and blame them by name (in writing), for what went wrong.

The above procedures will predictably cause a poor ranking and rating and a poor review that can justify "corrective" action. Once this happens, employees become disillusioned and many will leave Intel on their own, rather than suffer the final indignity of being terminated involuntarily.

For a competent professional with pre-Intel work experience, it's strange to observe many Intel program and project managers functioning merely as Gantt chart administrators and not as domain experts who possess ownership and accountability for the initiatives they are leading. If you look at non-microprocessor product development, supply chain management, and customer relationship management, there is a history of inefficiency and poor productivity, including projects that have consistently stalled, missed key milestones in execution, or completely failed to deliver. Project managers in these areas are very skilled at taking orders from management but are lacking in the necessary skills to identify, drive, and deliver the *right things*. Additionally, they either lack intestinal fortitude or have been conditioned to not challenge unrealistic demands coming from the delegating managers who don't dig into details, even on an as-needed, deep-dive basis. Sadly, when the culture rewards you for being servile instead of pushing back with frank discussion or taking risks to address problems at the root, then you will never be able to deliver the systemic solutions that are required to truly improve business processes and operational performance.

The essence of servility is unquestioning compliance with management desires. Servile behavior is driven by employees' desires to get good performance reviews and promotions. Let's face it, everyone wants to look good in the eyes of their manager. But at Intel, the anomaly is that the behaviors driving an individual's performance are precisely what's hurting operational performance. The problem with servile behavior, according Frank Muehleman from Dell, is that "if you hire people who are fine at taking direction but have no ideas of their own, they don't enhance the company much."[78] What suffers the most, then, is innovation: servile employees don't innovate. The result is that actions which ought to serve the good of the company give way to actions that only serve the individual.

---

[78] *Business Week* Online, "Hire People Better than You," June 20, 2005.

## VALUES SUMMARY

Behavioral inflection point led to actions and unspoken values that were the *antithesis* of the following Intel Values:

### RISK TAKING
⇒ Listen to all ideas and viewpoints
⇒ Embrace change and challenge the status quo

### QUALITY
⇒ Do the right things right
⇒ Continuously learn, develop and improve

### GREAT PLACE TO WORK
⇒ Manage performance fairly and firmly
⇒ Be open and direct

### DISCIPLINE
⇒ Conduct business with uncompromising integrity and professionalism
⇒ Pay attention to detail

### RESULTS ORIENTATION
⇒ Assume responsibility
⇒ Constructively confront and solve problems

## BEHAVIORS SUMMARY

Grove-era survival gave birth to Intel's methods of differentiating employees. The following behaviors became the unspoken values:

⇒ Years of service, grade level, network, and servility equate to employee competence and worth
⇒ Entitlement in the Barrett era as a final reward for surviving the Grove era
⇒ Preserving the status quo

# Chapter 6

# Managing Upward: The New Discipline

...many executives are actively complicit in their own deception: They want to hear good news, even if sometimes it's not the truth. If your underlings tell you that things are on track, you can relax and take all the credit. But if they tell you they've run into serious problems and don't know how to fix them, as a leader you face not only the hard work of helping them solve those problems but also the grim prospect of delivering bad news to your own bosses—the board and the stock market.[79]

Jeffrey Pfeffer

There are no shortcuts to anywhere worth going.

Beverley Sills

Andy Grove started the employee mantra at Intel that you manage your own career. His intention was to create a learning organization where people could move around into jobs in other functional areas to broaden their experience and their skill sets. Unfortunately, the mantra took on new meaning after the behavioral inflection point where actions ceased to match the published Values. For employees—managers, in particular—it morphed into a rationale for gaming the system to enhance their own career trajectories, shortcutting the accountability and hard work required under normal competitive conditions.

In company environments where there are more pressures from external competition, typically there is more internal rigor in assessing an individual's performance and contribution to operational results related

---

[79]http://money.cnn.com/magazines/business2/business2_archive/2004/10/01/8186678/index.htm.

to the firm's competitiveness. Rigorous differentiation of individuals in specific positions is required to constantly innovate and drive performance to a higher level. Intel's lack of formidable competition during the growth era under Grove, coupled with its environment of managing your own career, created fertile ground for the formation and nurturing of a bureaucracy, along with the behaviors that constitute "managing upward" within that bureaucracy.

In the Intel of today, managing upward is a sanctioned *and* encouraged activity. Intel managers, on average, have fewer than two employees reporting directly to them, yet survey data show that they don't hold regular one-on-one or staff meetings. This is a minimal responsibility that the small size of their organizations would seem to allow plenty of time for, but it can be explained by the conjecture that their focus on managing upward takes priority over the real work of managing subordinates. During orientation, new hires are told they need to begin managing their careers by setting the agendas and controlling the discussions in their one-on-one meetings with their managers. Over time, after observing the behaviors of managers, employees eventually learn that within the Intel culture, managing upward is the critical hinge to upward mobility. Once employees recognize this tribal knowledge, their upward-managing actions turn into deceptive or gaming behavior—imitating that of longer-term employees—as they develop this skill that must be mastered if they are to effectively compete and advance their careers.

## Pull + Position + Perception → Promotion

Three behaviors, in particular, have become the badge for managing upward in the culture: creating pull, creating perception, and positioning oneself for promotion. We will elaborate on all three.

Creating "pull" in any organization has to do primarily with finding someone above you in the management hierarchy who can help you rise in that hierarchy.[80] In the authors' experience over the past 25 years, there have been few places where this phenomenon did not hold true, but creating pull has clearly become an art at Intel. It's not unusual for an employee to stay with the same manager for more than a decade and garner multiple grade-level promotions. In essence, the employee gets

---

[80] Laurence J. Peter, *The Peter Principle* (New York, NY, 1969), 37-42.

carried along for the ride. It's truly amazing to find out what grade level some people have attained at Intel; it changes one's perspective. Take the example of a new startup area, for instance, where an individual is tasked with doing certain things such as establishing a new IT support group. There is basic infrastructure that needs to be put in place to support applications. For example, if you purchase an enterprise license for software, you have to establish the hardware environment, do the installation, set up helpdesk support, and develop corresponding training and rollout of that training to the user base, among other things. This author was surprised to learn, in actually experiencing this scenario at Intel, that the manager, who had been in IT for quite some time, didn't have the foggiest idea of what needed to be done. It was shocking to find out what the manager's grade level was and to realize that he didn't have the basic knowledge to perform in the job he was in. This particular individual had "hitched his wagon" to a long-tenured Intel veteran who had "pulled" him along for the ride, giving him higher grade levels along the way. All the manager needed to do to get by was delegate to underlings.

The phenomenon of creating pull is critical but not essential to getting ahead at Intel; the other two "skills" are even more necessary and have to be done in the right sequence in order to create the optimum conditions for promotion. Positioning oneself and creating the perception of accomplishment are the mechanisms by which the culture of forced discipline under Andy Grove transformed into a culture of "how to game the system to garner promotions" under Craig Barrett. The lack of shared discipline fosters an environment that allows for, and even encourages, the existence of numerous diffused initiatives that perpetuate and increase Intel's physical and business process fragmentation. At the same time, these initiatives help conceal the fact that Intel is, in many areas, a grossly over-staffed bureaucracy. The environment creates a bonanza for scheming employees who capitalize on (often co-opted) ideas and position themselves to build headcount "kingdoms" by selling and driving "urgent" new programs. Creating the perception that more work is getting done strongly correlates to getting promoted. The greater the headcount you manage, the better are your chances of increasing your grade level.

Again, an example will illustrate how this process works. In one Intel group, an experienced new hire suggested that the organization launch a supply chain program to improve many of the group's fragmented business processes and data systems. When asked by middle and senior management to come up with a maximum number of employees required to support the proposed program, the unwitting employee said, "20, perhaps 25 if you stretch it." The answer, apparently, wasn't satisfactory, because the management chain asked the question repeatedly, as if they were seeking a larger number than the experienced-new-hire's modest estimate of required program personnel. Not long afterward, a Grove Survivor stepped up to co-opt the program idea, and went on to sell and launch the new program involving well over 200 employees. The Grove Survivor provided plenty of new opportunities—for several fellow Survivors who were able to *position* themselves into key roles within the program. Over the course of the program, these individuals created the perception that they were getting things done successfully, when in fact the program was spiraling out of control and would soon result in several failures. Despite their track record, these individuals were able to disguise the impending failures for senior management while garnering promotions and increased stature within the organization. The pattern of managing upward is well established: employees feed management exactly what is required to keep a program going until they get a favorable annual review or the desired promotions. They invariably leave the program once it becomes difficult, and then go off and start something new so they can avoid seeing the difficult work through to completion. The evasive behavior allows these people to divorce themselves from accountability for these programs.

Managing upward is perhaps the most damaging practice found within the layers of Intel management bureaucracy because it usually entails (1) filtering out the "bad news" that must be confronted head-on if the company is going to prosper over the long haul; (2) creating metrics that convey the perception that results have been achieved; and (3) relying on inordinate amounts of headcount (as well as brute force) to create the illusion that work is getting done. Because Intel's deep pockets and rising stock price have provided the luxury of throwing "bodies" at most problems in order to achieve the desired results, managing upward has continued to be the dominant behavior of the Grove Survivors.

Unfortunately, senior management remains blind to this practice because the bad news rarely makes it to them unfiltered, and their attention is then diverted to the next big problem that's spoon-fed to them by the same set of people. Thus, the Grove Survivors create a law of perpetual motion, an imaginary momentum that never leads to tangible, positive results. It's almost as if they conceive themselves as moving targets: "If we just keep moving, no one can take a shot at us and hit us." Through the skillful use of their positions as "go to" people for their superiors and their ability to craft spurious IMBOs[81] that they can consistently meet, they are able to create the perception of progress while they squander Intel's time, money, and resources. In the opinion of the authors, the amount of waste across the company probably runs into the hundreds of millions of dollars annually.[82]

## Perception: "It's all good...more is better"

Vestiges from the Grove era of "forced-discipline execution" still exist, giving senior management the illusion that Intel has a disciplined culture and providing the means for employees to give the impression they are disciplined, when in reality the culture has grown quite lax. Perhaps the two most prominent vestiges of Intel's era of forced-discipline execution are (1) "IMBOs" or Intel Management by Objectives, where a set of company objectives is imposed on, and then trickles down through, the rest of the company,[83] and (2) the "ZBB" or "zero based budget" process for determining funding, in which proposed programs that fall above the ZBB line will be supported, and ones that fall below the line may be cut.

Under Andy, these IMBOs would be reviewed for goal clarity and alignment with the corporate objectives. Under Craig Barrett, managerial employees were for the most part free to set or specify their own IMBOs, with their manager's approval, in response to their work group's IMBOs coming from above. This freedom meant that skilled spin-doctors could create their own "make-work" objectives, which they could then "game" in order to create the illusion that they were working hard and contributing to Intel in substantive ways. The practice of creating

---

[81] Intel Management by Objectives
[82] A figure in the hundreds of millions of dollars annually is not unreasonable when you consider the $1.5 billion cost savings Hewlett-Packard expects from the layoffs announced in July 2005. (See http://biz.yahoo.com/ap/050715/hp_jobs.html?.v=6)
[83] Tim Jackson, *Inside Intel* (New York, NY: Penguin Group, 1997), 176.

perceived results by completing IMBOs is one of the keys to getting ahead at Intel.

Similarly, the use of ZBB at Intel often supports attitudes that are wasteful or extravagant—"How much work can we propose 'above' the ZBB line?" (it's all good; more is better)—rather than efficient and lean: "Which of the proposals is not compatible with or does not complement our existing capabilities and support our corporate goals?" (so we can easily decide what to take off our plate). One marketing manager[84] lamented the product development environment in the Barrett era, where available funding was "peanut buttered" or spread across the proposed programs, leaving each program short on funding. (For example, instead of launching eight programs with a 100% funding level, Intel would launch 10 programs with 80% funding for each.) Moreover, once programs are in flight, rarely do they fail to get approval to proceed past the requisite program checkpoints, and even rarer is outright cancellation. Instead, Intel goes on a hiring binge to resource the under-funded programs or to patch resource holes that are discovered late. So much time is spent communicating, reviewing, and status reporting that work and innovation start following a curve of diminishing returns—or more frankly—grind to a standstill. This phenomenon of adding more headcount to accelerate project schedules was proven ineffective as far back as 1975, when Frederick Brooks showed in *The Mythical Man-Month* that "When a project is late, the surest way to make it even more late is to add more people to the project."[85] The hiring fails to fix the problem because new employees cannot ramp and integrate quickly enough into the program, so then features are cancelled halfway through the program, just to meet the roadmap deadlines. The outcome of this practice is that Intel ends up with highly paid engineering resources that are wasted.

The farther away you get from product development programs—for example, when you venture into programs within support organizations—the worse things become. In such areas, Intel's deep pockets have supported this "more is better" attitude, overconfidence, and the throwing of "good money after bad" to a degree unseen perhaps

---

[84] Employee name withheld to protect confidentiality.
[85] Frederick Phillips Brooks, *The Mythical Man-Month: Essays on Software Engineering* (Addison-Wesley, 1975)

in any other company, as Intel's senior managers, lost without the disciplinarian Andy Grove, are unable or unwilling to make tough decisions or hold their fellow Grove Survivors accountable for even the most egregious, wasteful failures. It has become a game where people cycle through plan budgets to fund big programs that are supposed to "transform" Intel, when in reality these programs are merely a means of furthering the career trajectories of the entitled class, or those seeking to become part of it.

Andy Grove was a stickler for accountability, and by virtue of accountability, individuals were forced to measure and improve performance. This was especially true in manufacturing; it was less so (even then) in the support organizations, where performance is more susceptible to manipulation because it is more remote from unambiguous measures of product performance. Once the reins were handed over to Craig Barrett, the discipline around accountability waned quickly.

Almost everything that has been stated up to this point has focused primarily on individual behavior; however, logic dictates that if everyone in a division or organization is gaming the system, then the organization is doing it as well. Gaming the system has become the new discipline not only for individuals, but also for whole groups. Over the last five years it has become more apparent to the authors that Intel organizations have become hollow, as if their sole purpose were to game the performance management system (the goal being employee bonuses) rather than do those things that are for the overall good of the company. This new "discipline" (careerism) has made it difficult for the company as a whole to act in a truly disciplined and focused fashion. In light of the stagnant stock price, people have assigned accountability for gains (profit) to themselves, and this has superseded accountability for projects that drive operational performance. In essence, too many of Intel's people work for themselves and not for Intel. They try to make up for the flat stock price by getting promotions, which will yield them higher salaries and larger bonuses. While this may seem normal at many companies and certainly occurred in the Grove era, it appears to have become much more prevalent throughout the Barrett era and continues under Paul Otellini's leadership. Although Paul Otellini has eliminated organization-specific employee bonus goals, creating for the entire company only one, which is intended to foster more cooperation among employees and organizations, this action has not yet changed the behaviors.

Consistent with the attitude that "it's all good…more is better" and the over-use of delegation as described earlier (in "Management Process under Craig Barrett"), there has been an unfettered spawning of internal strategists and support organizations staffed by individuals filling various non-value-added roles. The strategists or others with glorious titles are really surrogates for the functional managers who have abdicated their right and responsibility to improve business processes for their respective domains. Instead, designated strategists spend most of their time in lengthy business process strategy meetings where months and months fly by as the team attempts to envision the perfect "end state." However, "When [these people are] confronted with a problem, [they] act as if discussing it, formulating decisions, and hashing out plans for action are really the same as actually fixing it."[86] When the design milestones are completed, a multi-year effort will then be launched to implement the "end-state" vision. It's comical, and yet sad, to see such a pervasive lack of focus and discipline, which allows so much energy to go into designing the nuances of a potential or *distant*-future business process, while at the same time, the team is unable to take tangible action to improve things within the next month or quarter and thus make step-by-step progress toward the "end state." Within the industry, there are many continuous improvement methodologies (Lean, Six Sigma, etc.) available to these managers and strategists, but adopting them would mean that these people would have to learn them and then, heaven forbid, actually do the real work.

Several interesting phenomena occur as a result of this odd state of affairs. For starters, new inductees into the culture, upon witnessing the "design overdose" or "analysis paralysis" cycle in action, will experience shock or disbelief that such gross inefficiency and ineffectiveness rule in a company whose public image remains that of a highly disciplined paragon of operational efficiency. When these employees engage with other companies to benchmark business processes, projects, or programs in order to improve them, participants from other companies, upon learning of Intel's team approach and lack of apparent management leadership, ask questions like, "What do your [functional] managers do if all of you [strategists] are doing the business process design work?" At

---

[86] "The Smart-Talk Trap," *Harvard Business Review*, May-June 1999, 136.

those same gatherings, Intel inductees will likely interact with functional managers from other companies, sometimes very senior-level managers, who are able to discuss their business processes and related improvement initiatives at a very, very detailed level. But the newcomers rarely find such detailed knowledge among Intel's senior, let alone middle managers, except perhaps in the area of fab process technology development.

Intel's flock of strategists, in effect, are full-time *internal* management "consultants" who generally get paid a lot more than the employees who work in the trenches and are held accountable for successfully executing the fragmented business processes that these consultants have been unable to fix or improve. Besides being wasteful and taking ownership (and accountability) from functional managers, these insider-consultants, having grown up within Intel's legendary "not invented here" culture, possess limited awareness of (or have even shunned) business methods and solutions that have proven successful at other companies, which could lead to dramatic improvements if applied to Intel's circumstances. It's reasonable to ask whether the prevalence of these "consultants" masks an ugly reality: how *could* most of Intel's functional managers have progressed without the discipline of a step-by-step, intra-functional, professional development process of the kind normally required to become a competent leader in one's field?

It is widely understood that having managers who know the intimate details of the business is a great safeguard against smart talk.[87] This explains why GE early on adopted the Six Sigma framework: they realized that with Six Sigma came accountability for operational performance within functional business areas. Since it appears that Intel is rife with smart-talking individuals, then it is logical to conclude that Intel's functional managers delegate accountability because they don't know the details of their business—or, if they did know the details at one time, it was 15 or 20 years ago when they were in the trenches, executing inefficient, ad hoc business processes. Without the safeguard of personally knowing the business and having a clear vision of how it should be run, these managers get overrun by the stampede of smart-talking sycophants and well-meaning but inept analysts that have infested much of Intel's unfocused, undisciplined culture.

---

[87] Ibid, 139-40.

Of course, having this disproportionately high number of program and project personnel—analysts, architects, strategists, and so forth—means you have constant role ambiguity and turf battles. In this fluid environment, personnel can quietly and quickly slide away from efforts that are beginning to crumble and likewise glom onto others that are experiencing even the smallest measure of success. This becomes very evident as you read status reports from many different individuals, all reporting on the same project, even if most of those doing the reporting are only remotely connected to the effort. They'll receive an employee's monthly report and add their own "twist" to what's in it, so it will appear that they've significantly contributed. Yet when a real problem needs to be solved, there never seem to be enough of the right "workers" to get the job done, though managers will eagerly volunteer to leverage their network and "crack the whip" in order to get things moving. This entire comedic scene is depicted in the cartoon above, entitled *Stuck in Mud*. The creation of a rank-and-file employee, it provides a humorous peek into the realities of Intel's culture outside of its core manufacturing competency, and highlights one of the steps that Intel managers master in order to position themselves upward for eventual promotion—maybe even to vice president.

## The Pull to Vice President

Years of observation and confirmation from several long-time employees suggest that an unwritten rule of entitlement at Intel is this: that once your staff headcount reaches 500, you will be promoted to a vice-president (VP) position, provided that the differentiation criteria are also met. (The authors know of one instance where a person was promoted to VP despite having only 400 people reporting to him). It often comes as a surprise to others within an organization when a person who's not noted for exceptional talent and hasn't left a trail of impressive tangible results becomes a vice president. At Intel, the most important ingredient for becoming a vice president, other than grade level, is having a large number of employees report to you. The more headcount you manage, the greater the perception of your importance and responsibility. Any evaluation of the results of your department is secondary to the focus on how many people there are in your department. Therefore, the authors offer the "rule of 500"—have at least 500 people reporting to you—as a criterion for becoming a vice president at Intel, outside of manufacturing. One would think that years of service would play the major role here, but there are some examples—very few, mind you—that defy the years-of-service rule. However, there are few examples to defy the rule of 500.

Within manufacturing, the formula becomes a little more complicated. In addition to the rule of 500, you must also have 20 or more years at Intel and, at one point in your career, you must have been a fab manufacturing manager, more often than not in New Mexico. Exceptions to these criteria for VPs in manufacturing occur only in the last category: a VP might have come up through the development fabs in either

California or Oregon, or be a long-time employee who resided overseas and rose through the ranks in the assembly and test manufacturing organization.

Otherwise, observation has shown that as long as you maintain the status quo (don't rock the boat), demonstrate some ability to crack the whip and get things done (even if it's through brute force), and effectively manage upward, then the path to becoming a VP is open, provided the other criteria have been met. By contrast, anyone who attempts to show that "the emperor has no clothes" with respect to the fragmentation of Intel's business processes (thereby getting in the way of individuals who are on the "path to VP") is easily marginalized or moved out of the way.

Indeed, the real gaming begins once an individual becomes a VP, because that will be followed by jockeying among employees to become the VP's technical assistant (TA). The TA positions are most coveted as a way of getting into the "leadership pipeline." Becoming a TA doesn't guarantee that you will become a VP, but it does give you entry into the game. There are many examples of people who've gone on to become VPs from TA positions, and the TAs who don't become VPs usually end up with "gravy train" positions within the Intel bureaucracy. These individuals expend a fair amount of energy finding a position that doesn't have too many direct reports and has little accountability. Once there, they spend their energy creating the perception that they are "influencing" whatever gets accomplished under their watch, but their work is usually of little or no consequence to the company. In other words, they do the right amount of nothing.

If the positions of most former TAs were eliminated, it is most unlikely that the reduction would negatively affect Intel's operational performance; rather, the effect would be positive because the company would save on the huge salaries these people get for negligible work. Moreover, TAs and the like have the detrimental effect of keeping "world beaters" with innovative ideas, technical competence, and the ability to execute from climbing the ladder of advancement within the company. They constitute a repressive "club" that sustains its highly paid existence by creating the perception of its value to the VPs, yet their existence is also one of "co-opetition." They jockey with fellow Grove Survivors for position and "face time" before VPs, while at the same time they cooperate with their network to suppress any competitive threats coming from people beneath them who do not belong to their club.

The culture of collective discipline at Intel has morphed into a culture of individual disciplined action that is channeled into advancing careers, while nowhere near the same level of focus is applied to facing realities and making decisions that are consistent with improving Intel's operating performance. Thus, many positions and organizations at Intel are hollow, displaying the symbols of discipline and competence, when in reality they sorely lack both.

## Summary

As unlikely as it may seem from perspectives outside the company, the Intel of today suffers from the damaging conditions discussed above: the loss of disciplined leadership; the rise of a culture of entitlement driven by delegation and avoidance of details concerning real problems; the prevalence of a "more is better" attitude that spawns countless diffused programs; and the proliferation of management roles filled by unfocused or irresolute individuals. Just as a cult dies with the passing of its leader, so has Intel's widespread discipline waned in the years following Andy Grove's tenure as CEO. Although consistently high revenue and earnings mask and perpetuate the lack of discipline that prevails in hollow support organizations outside of Intel's core competencies, and although symbols of discipline still exist (IMBOs, ZBB, etc.), one wonders if the "rubber-band discipline" will slacken even more, bringing further erosion of the Intel culture and with it further weakening of operational performance, now that Andy Grove has turned the board chairmanship over to Craig Barrett.

**VALUES SUMMARY**

The leadership actions of the Grove Survivors continue to perpetuate the *antithesis* of the following Intel Values:

**RISK TAKING**

⇒ Foster innovation and creative thinking

⇒ Embrace change and challenge the status quo

⇒ Listen to all ideas and viewpoints

**QUALITY**

⇒ Do the right things right

**GREAT PLACE TO WORK**

⇒ Work as a team with respect and trust for each other

**DISCIPLINE**

⇒ Make and meet commitments

⇒ Pay attention to detail

**RESULTS ORIENTATION**

⇒ Set challenging and competitive goals

⇒ Assume responsibility

⇒ Constructively confront and solve problems

⇒ Execute flawlessly

**BEHAVIOR SUMMARY**

The predominant behaviors of the Intel culture described in this chapter:

⇒ Managing Upward

⇒ Driving personal agendas for personal gain

⇒ Not working as a team that respects and trusts each other

⇒ Groupthink

# Chapter 7

# The Grip of Bureaucracy

Bureaucracy, the rule of no one, has become the modern form of despotism.[88]

Mary McCarthy

When everyone thinks alike, nobody thinks.

Anonymous

In January 2003, after spending 24 years at Intel, a retiring vice president was asked, "What challenges do you see in the coming years, and what does the future of Intel look like in the next 23 years?" Her response revealed what may be Intel's biggest obstacle as it tries to become a $70 billion company.

> I actually think the biggest challenge we have is realizing that a "lean and mean" organization will be necessary to compete in the world market. We have been fortunate to have great margins in our core business. While I would never want us to be in a commodity business, I do think it is important to be able to compete in those businesses if needed. Over the last 10 years it really does feel like our infrastructure is beyond what is really needed. Frequently I attend meetings where three or four management levels are necessary to make a decision, or where individual's jobs are so narrowly defined that it takes four to five people to get to the right answer, with each afraid to venture outside of their narrow field. We used to spend time at Intel asking ourselves what each function or position would do for the customer, to try to eliminate bureaucracy, and I believe we ought to consider this again. Time and again I hear people down in the organization questioning why we have so many two-in-the-boxes for no obvious reason, complaining that their jobs were more interesting when their responsibilities were broader,

---

and wondering why there are so many non-value-added steps in our processes.[89]

The observations of this vice president highlight the reality that Intel has had a growing bureaucracy filled with managers that are not effective at 'growing' the company efficiently. One way to look at efficiency is to look at headcount relative to operating income.

Data to Support Growing Bureaucracy and Diminished Operating Efficiencies in Barrett Era

| | End of Grove Era (1997) | End of Barrett Era (2004) | Increase (Decrease) | Percent Change |
|---|---|---|---|---|
| Corporate Leaders | 106 | 186 | 80 | 75% |
| Total Employees | 63,700 | 85,750 | 22,050 | 35% |
| Revenue | $ 25,070 | $ 34,209 | $ 9,139 | 36% |
| Operating Income | $ 9,887 | $ 10,130 | $ 243 | 2% |
| Operating Income per Corporate Leader | $ 93 | $ 54 | $ (39) | -42% |
| Operating Income per Employee | $ 0.155 | $ 0.118 | $ (0.037) | -24% |

All $ figures in millions

Taken from Intel Annual Reports, 1996-2005

The table above shows snapshots of the ends of both the Grove and Barrett eras. At the end of the Grove era, operating income per employee was $155,000, while at the end of the Barrett era it was $118,000, or 24% less. Thus, although operating income was $243 million higher at the end of the Barrett era, the decrease in operating income per employee shows that it took more headcount to generate this marginal improvement in operating income—implying lower employee productivity. Similarly, by the end of the Barrett era, the number of corporate leaders had increased by 75%, yet the operating income per corporate leader had decreased by 42%. During the Grove era, there had been only six levels between the CEO and rank-and-file employees in the factory; this had more than doubled to 13 by the end of the Barrett era. These two data points alone imply decreased efficiency in management and a gross increase in bureaucracy from the end of the Grove era to the end of the Barrett era.

One could argue that Grove led the company through the greatest boom in the PC market and Barrett led the company during the worst downturn. Leaders must respond to the changes in the marketplace, and it is clear that what Andy Grove did as a leader was appropriate. However, one would have to question whether Craig Barrett responded appropriately to the market forces during his tenure. The PC market

---

[89] Intel employee website.

clearly had matured; average selling prices were much lower than they'd been in the Grove era. Furthermore, in an employee webcast during the downturn, Barrett told employees that revenue and profit levels were at the same levels as 1997 but that Intel had 20,000 more headcount, clearly signaling that he was at least partially aware of Intel's bloated status. This market context should have driven different management behaviors with respect to employee productivity and operational effectiveness. That era would have been an opportune time to flatten the management structure, clean out the ranks of under-performing managers, and position the company for a leaner operating environment. Unfortunately, this did not happen.

The observations at the beginning of this chapter by the former Intel vice president makes it clear that employees know the company is top-heavy, and that as a result, it is less focused on customers and less employee-friendly. Intel's customers and suppliers are also aware of the company's growing bureaucracy. During an informal, off-the-record conversation, one senior executive at a supplier to Intel bemoaned the "layers and layers at Intel we have to deal with," adding that "no one in the industry likes to do business with Intel."[90] Comments like these from Intel's employees and partners make it clear that Intel has grown into an inward-looking bureaucracy.

## Growth in Bureaucracy

It has been the authors' observation that the bureaucracy's growth is fueled by two primary factors. The first is the practice of managing upward for personal gain, and the second is the existence of complex "matrix management" relationships among functional managers, program managers, and their respective teams. This has created an environment that is ripe for subversion and playing to political agendas. It has created a maze of inefficiency with respect to implementing change and executing results. It has become noticeable across practically every organization and has even presented symptoms publicly, in the form of product glitches and slips.

As we've shown, managing upward has become an art among the entitled class. Individuals who are adept at it position themselves to become the directors or general managers of product groups and increase

---

[90] Supplier name and company information withheld to preserve confidentiality.

the headcount they manage. Consequently, product teams have gotten much, much larger but not more efficient in generating products or reducing the cycle times to introduce them. The overwhelming focus is on securing the next promotion rather than reducing the cycle time of product introduction, growing market segment share, and driving financial and operational efficiency.

Given the broad range of markets that Intel competes in, a manager has to intimately understand the basis for competing in a given market, factors such as time-to-market, supply chain cost, service and delivery models, and customer profitability, among other things. This is absolutely critical for entry into new markets and can mean extinction for companies that aren't leaders in a mature market. Unfortunately, if managers are predominantly focused on pleasing their superiors by managing upward, they tend to lose focus on what's operationally important: they may delegate work without really understanding or monitoring whether progress is made; they might create metrics that look like progress but mask operational realities; and if they over-delegate in operational matters, they create opportunities for those below to also play the game of managing upward. The cross-functional interactions that should represent collaboration toward achieving a common goal become focused on team structure and decision authority: more time is spent determining what team structure should look like and who should have decision authority than on what work needs to be done.

## Lack of Accountability

Within the Intel bureaucracy, decisions are made by committee because many managers are insecure (for fear of reprisal) or generally directionless. Our observations have led us to conclude that two factors contribute to this phenomenon. The first has to do with managers not determining realistic, executable strategic direction. The second is that these same managers abdicate responsibility for executing strategy (especially when it's not executable) without abdicating authority for changing it. This is most likely to occur when program teams uncover operational deficiencies or previously unacknowledged market realities, such as the recent customer concern about heat dissipation in CPUs and servers. That particular market reality was first acknowledged and addressed by AMD, and only later by Intel—once AMD started gaining market share in these segments. As indicated earlier, many of the program manager positions are revolving doors for Grove Survivors, who pass through many programs while escaping accountability for the emerging failures or slips of the programs left behind. They delegate execution to employees, who get stuck in a turnstile, held accountable for executing strategies that may be neither feasible nor financially rewarding, yet which they are powerless to change because they lack decision authority.

Program managers who have delegated accountability because they're not familiar with what's required to execute spend a lot of time talking amongst themselves, trying to make decisions that they can showcase as *future* benefits to the managers above them. This leads to multiple forums for making decisions about similar things, and when Grove Survivors eventually realize that, they create an over-arching committee to make the final decisions, which ultimately will be delegated down the chain for execution. The authors have observed that, especially with large programs, these decisions have often been wrong not only for the programs, but for the company.

When you have an environment in which decisions are made by committee, coupled with revolving doors in the program management positions, you end up with a lack of accountability. Countless examples would illustrate this point, but to protect confidentiality, we will consider what happens at a high level. As a result of the hidden, moving targets for accountability, frustrated senior managers cannot find "a throat to choke" when things inevitably go wrong with programs; therefore, they vent their frustration by ambiguously assigning blame to the entire program team. With such a low level of individual accountability, no one person's position is at risk, so there are really no consequences for making bad decisions, even repeated bad decisions, and the shifting of program personnel recurs and the cycle begins anew.

The irony of this process is that, under the surface, there usually are one or two smart-talking individuals driving their own personal agendas and *influencing* the rest of the group to follow, thus creating false consensus.[91] There are several ways in which they accomplish this:

---

[91] "Hidden Flaws in Strategy," *The McKinsey Quarterly*, 2003, Number 2.

⇒ Confirmation bias – the tendency to seek out opinions and facts that support their beliefs and hypotheses.

⇒ Selective recall – the habit of remembering only facts and experiences that reinforce their assumptions.

⇒ Biased evaluation – the quick acceptance of evidence that supports their hypotheses, while contradictory evidence is subjected to rigorous evaluation and almost certain rejection; they often, for example, impute hostile motives to critics or question their competence (by pointing out their short tenure at Intel).

⇒ Groupthink – the pressure to agree with others in team-based cultures.[92]

These phenomena have become standard operating procedures, because so many people on the committees either lack the technical competence to come up with their own ideas or fail to challenge the smart-talkers, who come up with well-marketed but poorly-conceived ideas that are laden with half-truths. As Mark Twain astutely put it in his *Autobiography*, "We are discreet sheep; we wait to see how the drove is going, and then go with the drove." Because the bond shared by Grove Survivors is strong and the need to "stick together" is embedded in their DNA, decision making by committee, like managing upward, has become an art form. If a decision leads to failure, the one or two individuals who drove their own agendas quietly blend back into the group without being held personally accountable for their significant role in the failure, and then resurface when it's time to come up with a new plan or direction. At this point, they will comb the environment to find new ideas that may be gaining momentum among rank-and-file personnel, and they'll adopt these ideas as their own, once again driving them in the same direction, toward the same mistakes, that led to earlier rounds of failure. The behavioral pattern in which individuals *co-opt, corrupt,* and *cripple* good ideas becomes a characteristic pattern, a spiral that grows like a cancer, plaguing an increasing number of functional areas within Intel. Of the examples illustrating this phenomenon, the most notable and widely known are the repeated failures in the supply chain planning domain.

The authors have observed over the years, and emphasized in this book, that one of the critical factors lacking in many program managers is a necessary combination of technical competence and discipline of

---

[92] Ibid.

execution. In some cases these program managers may have technical competence but don't know how to execute, or alternatively, they may lack technical competence but know how to execute. On occasion, you will find program managers lacking both skills. (How they survive is anyone's guess!) Unfortunately, very little importance is placed on these two essential performance criteria in the domain of supply chain management, and this lack of emphasis contributes significantly to poor performance in that domain.

Take supply chain agility as an example. Intel has made numerous unsuccessful attempts to change the way production is planned, from spreadsheets to more advanced planning and decision-support applications. In the Grove era, *each leader who spearheaded an unsuccessful attempt "left" the company* after the project failed. However, throughout the Barrett era, each figurehead has remained at Intel after the project failed. The contrasting fates of supply chain planning project leaders speak volumes about how accountability has diminished in the post-1998 culture of entitlement at Intel. Regardless of the era, the reasons for project failure are many, yet they can usually be traced back to these overarching characteristics—a lack of domain-specific technical competence and a lack of ability to execute—in the project leaders.

The project leaders and participating organizations did not understand the root cause or nature of the underlying problems that needed to be fixed. Consequently, they formulated inappropriate strategies that violated fundamental principles for implementing supply chain planning systems, and these violations could not be overcome, no matter how many resources were thrown at the task (the project team at one point reached 300—enough to staff a good-sized microprocessor design team!). It reached the point where so many matrix management relationships existed that accountability for results became clouded, as if the group were cooperatively gaming the system in fear of being held accountable for their lack of technical competence. As the authors have shown, accountability without technical competence leads to decision making by committee, which in turn removes individual accountability from the people making the decisions.

Since Andy Grove withdrew from day-to-day affairs, there has been a significant leadership vacuum within many Intel organizations. One would think that many managers would be eager to step up to bat and prove their worth by personally filling the leadership vacuum. However, the opposite has been true. As highlighted by the retiring VP at the beginning of this chapter, Intel's response to this vacuum has been to create more layers of bureaucracy, more organizations co-managed by two managers, more highly-matrixed programs governed by committees rather than led by individuals, and more use of delegation, not only for executing to direction, but also for formulating strategy. The result of all this bureaucracy is an organization focused on keeping the wheels on the car, or maintaining the status quo. Any change to the status quo means that *everyone* has to agree to that change, and the only way to accomplish this is by consensus decision making, which is normally done by committee.

It seems that the main objective of senior and middle managers is to position themselves to make decisions and, if possible, get into decision-making positions on a committee even *before* they know what problems need to be solved, a clear sign that Intel is rife with bureaucracy. In fact, among the April Fool's jokes posted on the employee website in 2005 was a play on Moore's Law, which directly lampooned the growth of vice presidents at Intel: "Otellini's Law" stated that the number of vice presidents doubles every 18 months.[93]

Source: Intel Annual Reports 2000-2005

If you visually stack all the vice presidents across the five platform groups, you have the shape of an airplane. It's reminiscent of the movie *Wall Street,* when Gordon Gecko refers to the passing around of memos by all the vice presidents of Teledyne Paper as one of the reasons why overhead is so high. Intel management justifies the number of vice

---

[93] Intel Employee Website, April Fool's edition, 2005.

presidents based on the number of people in the company, instead of basing it on profit and loss operational groups.

## Dealing with Bureaucracy

To date, Intel has proven to be ineffective in dealing with its mammoth bureaucracy. This shortcoming provides another profound contrast between Intel and GE. In GE's 2000 annual report, Jack Welch did not mince words when he said:

> We cultivate the hatred of bureaucracy in our Company and never for a moment hesitate to use that awful word "hate." Bureaucrats must be ridiculed and removed. They multiply in organizational layers and behind functional walls—which means that every day must be a battle to demolish this structure and keep the organization open, ventilated and free. Even if bureaucracy is largely exterminated, as it has been at GE, people need to be vigilant—even paranoid—because the allure of bureaucracy is part of human nature and hard to resist, and it can return in the blink of an eye. Bureaucracy frustrates people, distorts their priorities, limits their dreams and turns the face of the entire enterprise inward.[94]

The use of Six Sigma by GE has been an effective tool to keep the organization focused on customers and operational improvements, rather than on its own machinations. If you are buried under or work within a bureaucracy, then Jack Welch's words are music to your ears. He gives powerful reasons why eliminating bureaucracy is critical to the health of any organization (to keep it open, ventilated, and free) and warns that "people need to be vigilant" in the everyday "battle to demolish" bureaucracy. Later in this same annual report, he identifies the specific types or classifications used to differentiate managers, so that the right people are rewarded and the wrong people—especially the "kiss up and kick down" bureaucrats—are removed in order to preserve the company culture and drive higher performance. Although the following excerpt is long, it's so powerful and so relevant to Intel that we feel it must be included:

> [Leadership is] about the four "types" that represent the way we evaluate and deal with our existing leaders. Type I: shares our values; makes the numbers—sky's the limit! Type II: doesn't share the values; doesn't make the numbers—gone. Type III: shares the values; misses the numbers—typically, another chance, or two.

---

[94] Annual Report, General Electric, 2000, 5.

None of these three are tough calls, but Type IV is the toughest call of all: the manager who doesn't share the values, but delivers the numbers; the "go-to" manager, the hammer, who delivers the bacon but does it on the backs of people, often "kissing up and kicking down" during the process. This type is the toughest to part with because organizations always want to deliver—it's in the blood—and to let someone go who gets the job done is yet another unnatural act. But we have to remove these Type IVs because they have the power, by themselves, to destroy the open, informal, trust-based culture we need to win today and tomorrow…

We made our leap forward when we began removing our Type IV managers and making it clear to the entire Company why they were asked to leave—not for the usual "personal reasons" or "to pursue other opportunities," but for not sharing our values. Until an organization develops the courage to do this, people will never have full confidence that these soft values are truly real. There are undoubtedly a few Type IVs remaining, and they must be found. They must leave the Company, because their behavior weakens the trust that more than 300,000 people have in its leadership.[95]

Under Jack Welch's leadership, GE experienced a period of outstanding performance. Removing bureaucracy and developing leadership were the lifeblood of performance improvements for GE, and it's clear from the excerpts above that these values are an integral part of its corporate culture. GE makes a daily, *conscious* effort to fight against bureaucracy. To help with this fight it has leaders who understand the details or at least aren't averse to them (so they can't be easily fooled), and it has developed an open, rigorous, unambiguous process for differentiating employees and cutting loose individuals who consistently fail to deliver meaningful results or live by the company values.

Sadly, the same cannot be said for Intel, where bureaucracy has grown and spread like cancer, choking innovation and impeding operational excellence throughout much of the company. Robert Noyce would roll over in his grave if he saw how the company he started—this "partnership of equals," designed to be egalitarian and not autocratic in nature—has morphed into an out-of-control aristocratic bureaucracy, where the power players trample the principles upon which Intel was founded.

---

[95] Ibid, 5-6.

## Evolution of Intel Culture

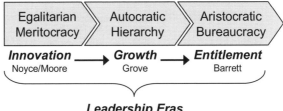

### The Culture Impedes Operational Excellence

As Intel entered 2004 and experienced a series of execution missteps, many rank-and-file personnel were sensitized—more than ever—to the damaging effects of the company's bureaucracy. They saw that bold, decisive executive action was probably going to be the only way to address this problem. These feelings had been brewing for several years and finally reached a peak in September 2004, when CEO Craig Barrett addressed employees via an "Executive Connect Webcast."

As far back as 2000, Barrett must have sensed a decline in the company's performance, for in the latter part of that year he launched a corporate "Operational Excellence" initiative. The mission of "OpX" was, and is, to "do a great job for our customers, employees and stockholders by:

- Driving flawless execution to world-class standards
- Making and meeting our commitments
- Being intolerant of mediocrity and bureaucracy
- Continuously improving in everything we do."[96]

While there are many facets to this "OpX" initiative, the one that grabbed employees' attention from its inception was the charge to be "intolerant…of bureaucracy." Many employees felt that Intel culture had changed for the worse because of a tremendous growth in bureaucracy.

The timing of the launch of OpX in 2000 could not have been better. Intel was arguably overstaffed because (1) it had recently added extensive headcount through acquisitions and external hiring during the dot-com boom, and (2) there was now a decrease in demand as the cyclical semiconductor industry entered its worst downturn in history,

---

[96] Intel employee website.

attributable to the dot-com bust. Many of the Grove Survivors who had seen the organization grow underneath them were now more vigorously jockeying for position, both individually and for the groups they ran, because the consolidation of acquisitions followed by a downturn meant that there was less actual work to be spread among the existing personnel. Moreover, many groups, particularly within support areas, were continuing to grow even during the downturn in order to support the corporate mission of becoming "the preeminent building block supplier for the Internet economy." The IT group, in particular, seized the opportunity to "transform" Intel by promising to make it more operationally efficient. The resultant growth in personnel, however, led to a growth in bureaucracy and decreased morale as employees, feeling less empowered, wondered if their individual contributions made a positive difference in the company.

Encouraged and emboldened by the company's pronouncements on OpX, many employees began to confront the problem of bureaucracy at Intel. They expected their direct managers to listen to and embrace their suggestions for eliminating bureaucratic processes. They thought that the corporate OpX program office would be hunting down and eliminating blatant bureaucracies. But to their surprise and disappointment, their attempts to address the problem were summarily dismissed or ignored. Out of frustration, some employees then attempted to bypass their direct managers and the OpX program office by elevating directly to senior management. Unfortunately, this usually resulted in senior management's passing on their complaints to the same subordinates within the bureaucracy who had rebuffed the employees' efforts in the first place.

Hopes for some impending, meaningful action to address Intel's bureaucracy began to rise again after a series of addresses by Craig Barrett in July 2004. First, a visibly angry Barrett addressed all employees after the second quarter (Q204) earnings were released. During this webcast, Barrett said the company had not fully adhered to its imperative to achieve Operational Excellence, as demonstrated by lower-than-forecast margins, a major product recall, and a decline in customer satisfaction ratings. He made it clear that all employees, including managers, needed to do a better job of living the Intel Values in order to improve company performance.

Second, Barrett addressed roughly 200 of Intel's most senior leaders and spoke bluntly about execution and performance; he spelled out exactly what he wanted these leaders and all employees to do. Interestingly, he mentioned that after the Q204 webcast to all employees he "didn't get one message back from them saying, 'Barrett, you're screwed up. We don't need to do this.' All that I got back were messages that said, 'God, it's about time. What's taken you guys so long?' So there are about 81,000 people that are waiting for us to do something." Barrett's response to the flood of employee feedback furthered employee hopes that meaningful actions to address bureaucracy would be forthcoming.

Finally, Barrett sent out an "open letter to Intel employees," reiterating that Intel's success depends on its "culture of Operational Excellence and our performance to values such as Discipline, Results Orientation, and Customer Orientation." The fact that this open letter became public when it was leaked to the outside world only heightened employees' anxiety over what they saw as a weakening corporate culture and a plain-as-day need to remove "kissing up and kicking down" or grossly under-performing managers who routinely violated the Intel Values.

Late in the third quarter of 2004, on the tail of these three messages from Barrett, the hallway talk about Intel's decaying culture was reaching a peak. Rank-and-file employees were more eager than ever to see senior managers take steps toward eliminating Intel's staggering and stifling bureaucracy. It was in this setting that rank-and-file employees again reached out to senior management, in anticipation of the September 2004 worldwide Executive Connect Webcast with Craig Barrett. Not surprisingly, the Webcast set new records for attendance and participation, with a grand total of 10,580 Intel employees submitting 1,888 questions, for which Barrett had time to answer about 70. These tallies *significantly* eclipsed previous records in the Executive Connect program's two-year history. There were questions ranging from write-offs of the $10 billion in acquisitions to the poor execution of product roadmaps, but the paramount theme of the questions was rank and file's continued frustration with the growing bureaucracy and the apparent lack of accountability for mistakes made repeatedly by middle- and senior-management personnel. In fact, one questioner explicitly asked if Intel's executive staff would consider adopting an approach like GE's to identify and remove values-violating, non-performing managers. Another bluntly asked if "heads roll" at Intel.

In response to these questions, Craig Barrett claimed that the company's performance management process (focal) effectively dealt with problem personnel, adding that those who "repeat mistakes" should "obviously" be disciplined, no matter what their level in the company, and "that sort of discipline could include termination." However, he also said that he didn't favor "public hangings" and had disagreed with the recent firings of three Hewlett-Packard vice presidents who had repeatedly missed quarterly revenue targets.

> One example of how Intel fires someone is that of the "retiring" vice president for the Wireless Communications group. Employees were told that this vice president was retiring after a long, "stellar" career at Intel. The reality was that not only had the division taken a $600 million goodwill write-down for the quarter, but this vice president had thought it a good idea to raise prices on flash products by 40% during a constrained supply situation (in typical Intel fashion, taking the screws to the customer).
>
> The impact on Intel was a double whammy: the write-off contributed to a loss for the quarter, and the 40% price increase lost Intel its largest customer. This mistake was public, so it was no coincidence that this vice president had to "retire." Management tried to hide the bungling rather than be honest with employees and tell everyone that the vice president had been fired.
>
> What's important about this story is that it took something of *significant* magnitude that had *public* impact to get rid of an entitled person. Had there been no "double whammy" in the flash division, this vice president would probably still be working at Intel.
>
> The essence of Barrett's leadership is that failure has no consequences unless it is publicly visible and hits profits hard. However, even that isn't consistently true. Intel Communications Group has lost money for four out of the five years of its existence under the leadership of one vice president, who is still with the company. It isn't clear what these senior managers are held accountable to with respect to strategic and

financial objectives. Under similar circumstances, any other company would replace them.

| Operating Income for ICG (Acquisitions) | | | | |
|---|---|---|---|---|
| 2000 | 2001 | 2002 | 2003 | 2004 |
| $ 319 | $ (735) | $ (817) | $ (824) | $ (791) |

Taken from Intel Annual Reports, 2000-2004

Barrett's answers to these questions *sounded* good at face value, but they were not consistent with management actions. The problem, as we've shown, is that the managers in the entitled class, including executive management, generally have an aversion to details that keeps them from developing the discernment necessary to see when personnel are repeating mistakes, violating Values, "spinning," "brute forcing" unsustainable results, or manipulating the non-financial numbers to make themselves look good. Rank-and-file personnel and most of the newer employees (nearly one half of Intel employees have been with the company fewer than six years) *do* live in the details and therefore *are* generally able to discern these inappropriate behaviors; consequently, they are beside themselves with indignation over senior management's inability and unwillingness to remove such people from the organization, when it should be blatantly obvious what needs to be done.

Barrett's feckless responses at the September 2004 webcast and subsequent inaction made it abundantly clear that he was not going to make good on his commitment to take bold action commensurate with his previous comment that "there are about 81,000 people that are waiting for us to do something." His inaction in the face of a cultural crisis exemplifies Intel's pervasive inability to identify and properly respond to current realities.

Was this inaction due to lack of understanding, lack of intestinal fortitude, a case of senior management denial, or a combination of all the above? It's difficult to tell for certain, but one thing is clear: Craig Barrett's inaction did not meet employees' expectations but rather dashed any hopes that they had of seeing a meaningful improvement to the culture. During the earlier downturn, the right move would have been to sell off unprofitable divisions, pare headcount, and make Intel lean and mean again. Instead, when revenue growth returned in 2003, Intel continued to grow headcount. As Winston Churchill pointed out, "there is no worse mistake in public leadership than to hold out false hopes soon to be swept away."[97]

## Employees Are Not Fools

What makes Barrett's late-2004 inaction all the more poignant is the environment in which it took place. In February 2004 a firestorm had erupted within Intel regarding the health of its vaunted culture, especially with respect to the freedom of Intel employees to "constructively confront" the status quo or elevate bad news without fear of reprisal. It all started at Intel's 2004 International Sales and Marketing Conference. Andy Grove, chairman of Intel's board of directors, posed the following question to the 3,000 employees in attendance: "Has Intel culture changed?" During the ensuing roundtable discussion, employees argued that their efforts to speak up had been largely ignored and sometimes punished by managers, leading many employees to censor themselves and eventually give up in their efforts to constructively confront important issues facing their organizations.

The following week, news of this roundtable discussion was published in a feature article on Intel's employee website. The article generated a tremendous number of email follow-up questions and opinions from employees worldwide. Most emails published in the "letters to the editor" section of the website came from rank-and-file personnel and, for the most part, corroborated the claims of Sales and Marketing employees who had spoken out at the roundtable. In fact, the intensity and volume of emails were so great that eight days later, the employee website ran another feature article on Intel culture, this time an interview with CEO Craig Barrett and then-Chief Operating Officer (COO) Paul Otellini. In this interview, both Barrett and Otellini rejected employees' claims that the Intel culture had changed; they insisted that it was as strong and vibrant as ever.

It was from this beginning that employees began receiving what appeared to be a regular diet of company propaganda extolling the virtues and strength of Intel's culture and encouraging employees to live by the Intel Values. Through various media, employees were repeatedly told that Intel's culture was not changing or weakening; rather, what seemed to them like a cultural problem with challenging the status quo was merely a "bi-directional communication problem" where employees

---

[97] Winston Churchill, *The Hinge of Fate* (Boston: Houghton Mifflin, 1950), 61.

and their managers were not clearly communicating each other's expectations. Personnel were also encouraged to adhere to the Intel Values and were assured that they could simply solve the bi-directional communication problem by working with their managers to make sure that the bad news coming from below was comprehended. Most employees, on the other hand, were (and still are) convinced that the problem goes much deeper than a mere "communication problem" and are frustrated by what they believe are out-of-touch senior managers and intractable middle managers who give off signals that they really don't want to know the truth and will punish you if you keep confronting them with reality.

Those who stay at Intel respond in various ways; some are completely disillusioned and become disengaged, while others find relief through biting humor. Perhaps the best example of the latter occurred on April Fool's Day of 2005, particularly in the article referred to earlier, which expressed employees' disgust with the entitlement culture and growth in bureaucracy by nodding to Moore's Law: "Otellini's Law" states that "the number of vice presidents at Intel will double every 18 months." This same article lampooned Intel's practice of "two-in-a-box" management by saying "If Intel had been this successful in the past, with only two vice presidents for many key positions, just imagine how well we will do with four, eight, even sixteen-in-a-box." Most average employees know that growth in the number of Intel managers and vice presidents has outstripped revenue and employee growth, and this is just one case where humor provided a safe outlet for decrying the company's mushrooming bureaucracy.

Earlier in 2005, Intel had published the "Intel Culture Poster" as an additional means to reinvigorate the Intel culture. This document was not intended to replace the venerable Intel Values, but rather to help put them into action. The poster was created based on organizational health data, employee feedback, and senior leaders' discussions. Four improvement areas were identified:

- Risk taking and innovation,
- Open and direct communication,
- Manager effectiveness,
- Operational excellence.

Few Intel employees disagreed with the validity of these focus areas, but many recognized the countervailing realities that created genuine fear of reprisal (taking a risk that fails, being too open and direct with your manager or in exposing fallacious status quo thinking, etc.). So on April Fool's Day, a new "Intel Culture Poster" was published, and again, under the guise of humor, it appears that truth came forth.

| Official Culture Poster[98] | April Fool's Poster |
|---|---|
| **Our actions bring Intel Values to life.** | **Our inactions make Intel Values kind of sad.** |
| **Innovate.** *When we innovate, we advance.* We take informed risks to take advantage of opportunities. We seek creative ways to solve problems. We embrace change and challenge the status quo. | **Waffle.** *When we prevaricate, we buy time. Especially in meetings.* Sometimes not making a decision just feels right. Plus, sometimes we can keep people from getting mad at us. |
| **Communicate.** *When we communicate, we clarify.* We are open and direct. Always. We work towards constructive outcomes. We address what's tempting to avoid. | **Flatter.** *When we flatter, we make someone feel a trifle better at the expense of our dignity.* We believe inane platitudes might just distract participants from the conflict at hand. We try to sound like we mean it. Always. |
| **Manage.** *When we manage, we focus.* We keep our team focused on what's most important. We communicate our expectations. We provide constructive and timely feedback. | **Shirk.** *The easiest job of all is the one we don't bother to do.* When we slack off, we have more time for gaming. Nothing says "team" like making one sad schmuck do all the work. |

Almost unanimously, Intel rank-and-file employees would state that the 2005 April Fool's Day edition of the Intel employee website, which boldly lampooned Intel's culture and bureaucracy, was far and away the best in Intel's history. No doubt the humor struck a soothing, yet important chord with employees looking for decisive action to combat

---

[98] Intel's Employee website

Intel's bureaucracy and heal its ailing culture. But without the requisite management changes to fix Intel's culture, the joke is still on rank-and-file personnel.

Unfortunately, neither the September 2004 webcast with its tidal wave of questions nor the 2005 April Fool's Day satires on the employee website have prompted senior management to side with rank-and-file personnel in their view of the need to eliminate bureaucracy and align employee behaviors and culture with the published Intel Values. Yet this is the overarching problem affecting Intel's ability to sustain performance, and employees don't know how they could make themselves clearer. It seems that senior management is either in denial or believes that the culture can be cured without their making the toughest and most important decisions—those that deal with removing malfunctioning (or non-functioning) personnel. What management doesn't realize is that without the ability and *courage* to differentiate and cull all employees—including those in the entitled ranks—in a more scientific and robust fashion, Intel's bureaucracy will continue to flourish and conceal the bad news, out of self-interest. This will result in a continual weakening of Intel's culture as vital programs continue to falter.

Adherence to values is critical to the success of an organization. When you look at Intel's history, it is clear that people are the stewards of the Values. You could also say that Intel's compliance process with the Values has swung from being "ruthless" in the early years under Grove to being "toothless" in the entitlement era under Barrett. It would appear that the pendulum must find the appropriate middle ground: Intel must be more thorough in its management of performance to Values and synchronize them to metrics for operational performance, if the company expects to have the right personnel in place to properly respond to the marketplace realities it now faces.

## Values Summary

Adherence to the following Intel Values declined under the explosive growth of bureaucracy:

### Risk Taking

⇒   Learn from our successes and mistakes
⇒   Listen to all ideas and viewpoints
⇒   Embrace change and challenge the status quo
⇒   Foster innovation and creative thinking

### Quality

⇒   Achieve the highest standards of excellence
⇒   Do the right things right
⇒   Continuously learn, develop and improve

### Great Place to Work

⇒   Be open and direct
⇒   Recognize and reward accomplishments
⇒   Manage performance fairly and firmly

### Discipline

⇒   Make and meet commitments
⇒   Properly plan, fund and staff projects
⇒   Pay attention to detail

### Results Orientation

⇒   Set challenging and competitive goals
⇒   Focus on output
⇒   Assume responsibility
⇒   Constructively confront and solve problems
⇒   Execute flawlessly

### Customer Orientation

⇒   Make it easy to work with us
⇒   Deliver innovative and competitive products and services

## Behavior Summary

The predominant behaviors of the Intel culture described in this chapter:

⇒   Gaming the focal performance review system
⇒   Sycophantically managing upward
⇒   Groupthink
⇒   "Spinning" reality to paint rosy picture to management
⇒   Avoiding accountability by sticking together to hide lack of technical competence and ability to execute

# Chapter 8

# The Era of Denial

People are motivated to believe that things are great—so much so that they'll give off signals that they don't want the truth.[99]

Jeffrey Pfeffer

Any intelligent fool can make things better and more complex. It takes a genius and a lot of courage to move in the opposite direction. So often we tend to complicate things, perhaps thinking that the more complicated the analysis and eventual solution, the higher the value of the solution. In truth, it is often the simple solutions that harbor more value.

Albert Einstein

Doing the same old things in the same old way and expecting a different result. If we continue to operate in such a way that we refuse to learn from the past, not only are we condemned to repeat it, but we perpetuate a cycle of personal and professional failure. In the end, perhaps that is the true insanity.[100]

Rita Mae Brown

## Constructive Confrontation is Dead...Denial Rules

Intel is famous for its cultural hallmark of "constructive confrontation," the expectation that employees will confront problems in an open and direct way in order to ensure speedy resolution of those problems. This practice, started in the early days of Intel, is credited with

---

[99] http://money.cnn.com/magazines/business2/business2_archive/2004/10/01/8186678/index.htm.
[100] Quote of the day, www.excite.com.

helping the company maintain its competitive edge by enabling employees to make correct decisions that have kept Intel on top of the fast-moving high-technology industry for most of its history. However, the authors have lately observed that this cultural hallmark is all but dead.

> Andy Grove hosted a strategy meeting at Intel headquarters in December [2005]. Intel's famously demanding former chief quietly listened to executives politely pondering how Intel's microprocessors will be shaped by trends like Web computing. When the executives filed out, Grove stayed behind for a one-on-one meeting with Patrick Gelsinger, who runs its largest division: desktop and server chips. He's also a Grove protégé. Grove tore into him. He told Gelsinger that he didn't appreciate sitting through head-nodding meetings that lacked the drama of the old Intel. Where was the shouting? Who was challenging ideas and questioning data? Grove told Gelsinger he better shape up. 'He beat the tar out of me for not being confrontational,' says Gelsinger.[101]

If any rank-and-file employee were asked what has happened to constructive confrontation, the answer would be unanimous that it is still preached, but not effectively practiced. Rather, constructive confrontation is punished, especially when the one initiating it is a manager's subordinate or is employed at a lower grade level than the one receiving the request to participate in the meeting. Interestingly, the latest effort undertaken by Paul Otellini in July 2006 was to decrease the number of middle managers at Intel by firing about 1,000 of them. After interviewing many of these terminated managers, it has become apparent that many of them had one of two things in common. The first was that many of them were "known" to constructively confront the status quo (which sometimes means challenging your manager) only to suffer the final consequence of termination. The graphic below illustrates the approach taken. The second, and more interesting of the two, is that many long-time employees who were looking for a job change, ventured outside of their "network" within the last twelve-to-eighteen months into other business groups, only to realize that they were not part of the "new" network. They were thus viewed as outsiders, regardless of their tenure at Intel. In the new group, they became easy prey when their new management had to "make the numbers" for terminations. This calls into

---

[101] www.forbes.com/free_forbes/2006/0410/042.html?partner=yahoomag

question the power of the network for differentiation when one ventures outside of their established network.

*"Encouraging dissent is a good way of finding out who the traitors are."*

A former Intel project manager stated four years ago that "the only thing worse for an organization's health than *too much* confrontation is *no* confrontation."[102] In a culture of entitlement such as Intel's, however, you cannot practice constructive confrontation. In the early years of Intel, before the entitled class emerged, constructive confrontation was the norm and was very effective in driving people (and the company) to higher levels of performance. If Andy Grove's lashing of Pat Gelsinger can be taken as a stinging indictment of management's lack of adherence to the Intel Values, the decline of constructive confrontation becomes a second significant measure of Intel's faltering cultural health (the first measure being Barrett's statement in chapter 2 proclaiming that the health of the Intel culture could be gauged by the performance of Intel's products, because "product performance cannot lie"). The general absence of constructive confrontation in the Intel culture has been felt since the beginning of the Barrett era, but the encounter between Andy Grove and Pat Gelsinger marks the first instance of its becoming public with respect to a senior Intel manager. Like most employees, the authors believe that the lack of constructive confrontation is a clear sign that senior management is out of touch and that the company no longer has an effective mechanism for dealing with people, processes, and technology that hinder operational performance.

Paul Otellini, a pure product of the Intel culture, to date appears

---

[102] www.pminyc.org/files/PMI_Constructive_Confrontation.pdf, February 20, 2002.

unaware of this view of what Intel's culture has become. Now that he has taken the reins as CEO at Intel, he is faced with three key challenges to turn Intel back into a high-tech growth company. The first challenge is to penetrate newer, high-growth markets while preserving the average selling price and healthy margins of the CPU-based platforms. We will address this first challenge in chapter ten. The second challenge is that of overcoming the slow-moving bureaucratic behemoth that was once an agile organization under Andy Grove. This will be no small feat, because in the age of mass "consumerization," the goal is no longer brute-force production of mass quantities of microprocessors, but rather the ability to turn on a dime in order to meet finicky consumer whims that drive the markets Intel is targeting with its new platform initiatives. The third challenge, and probably the most difficult, is to restore confidence in the culture and the published Intel Values by *inspecting actual* behaviors and performance against those Values—which is to say getting personally involved, rather than just paying lip service to them or merely *expecting* everyone to live by them. This is especially important in the middle and senior management ranks.

This last challenge, if not addressed, could potentially be the beginning of the demise of Intel. This sounds very ominous, and it is. The morale of the rank and file is at its lowest point in years, yet management seems oblivious to this fact. There has been a brain drain of talented people from Intel over the last few years, especially the most talented of those who came to Intel from acquisitions. These are typically the kinds of people that a company does not want to lose, but they are leaving because they see no future at Intel. Stock price has been trading horizontally for years, and there are very few opportunities for promotion because of the slow business growth and the low turnover among the Grove Survivors, who are "staying put" at all costs and clogging the leadership pipeline.

In addition to the familial bond that drives a deep loyalty and provides protection within the Grove Survivor community, there is also a fear among senior management that if the long-time employees (Grove Survivors) leave or are removed, they will give away "competitive advantage" to their next employers. This has led to an obsession with retaining them by offering more stock options and higher bonuses. The unjustified paranoia over losing "survivors" to competition has triumphed over the need to remove them for their significant, recurring failures. Lacking sufficient orientation to detail, Intel management cannot (or does not want to) get an accurate picture of people's *individual* worth to the company (technical competence, ability to execute, etc.), so they assume it's better to retain the long-time employees than to let them go and risk the loss of potentially competitive information. It is the opinion of the authors that the destruction of the culture and the loss of truly talented personnel are far more damaging than the loss of potentially competitive information harbored by bureaucratic sycophants who violate company values and have been given a blank check to repeat mistakes *ad infinitum*. In reality, most Grove Survivors have been detached from the trenches of company operations for so long that they would only be giving up information that might have been competitive 10 to 15 years ago. On top of this, as we have observed, few of them have demonstrated the ability to execute and implement change: most delegate down the hierarchy until the buck reaches someone who is willing to exercise the Intel Value of taking a risk. Unfortunately, whatever reality is confronted will be filtered and diluted on its way back up to the top.

To date Paul Otellini has sent out mixed signals on where he stands with respect to Intel's bureaucracy. On one hand, he has done some modest "housecleaning" among the senior management ranks. According to the employee grapevine, he told Craig Barrett in early 2005 to take care of his "dirty laundry" before the CEO leadership transition in May of that year. As a result, several vice presidents who (arguably) were low on competence and job performance quietly departed during the months preceding the transition. For rank-and-file employees who were tapped into the grapevine, this 'news' provided a modicum of hope that Paul Otellini would take meaningful steps to fight against and clear out the bureaucracy that had grown to mammoth proportions during the Barrett era. On the other hand, after the selected VP departures, there were no follow up actions that would indicate Otellini was serious about fighting bureaucracy. Rather, the modest housecleaning appeared to be more about settling personal vendettas than fighting Intel's bureaucracy. These minimal actions, followed by inaction, merely left in their wake a host of disillusioned employees.

If these employees had paid closer attention to Paul Otellini's words, they might never have raised their hopes in the first place. Before his ascension to CEO, Otellini had made some revealing and highly discouraging comments with respect to bureaucracy and the Intel culture. In a January 2005 interview with *The Wall Street Journal*, Otellini was asked if he was concerned that some former employees say "the company has become more bureaucratic and politicized." In response, Otellini said, "Bureaucracy in and of itself is not bad. It runs things…We have 80,000 people, many of them technologists, most of them very bright. And you have this situation where these very bright people have competing ideas. I suspect that some of the people you talked to are people who thought their ideas should have won." [103]

Otellini's assessment of the situation is not entirely correct. As a member of the Grove Survivor network and a pure product of Intel's cultural devolution, he is oblivious of the extent to which decision making is dominated by Grove Survivors within Intel's bureaucracy. He fails to realize that the playing field for influencing decisions is not level because, over the years, entitled personnel have taken over the culture. While the *talk* of egalitarianism can still be heard throughout Intel, the *walk* is mostly gone.

Most Intel decision processes go through motions consistent with an egalitarian culture in that they allow all personnel (entitled class and expendable class) to attempt to live the Intel Values and do things like "challenge the status quo" with their ideas. They will be given space to air their ideas in various forums and in front of a wide variety of personnel, completely consistent with what would seem to be a level playing field. However, underneath this ostensibly egalitarian surface, where one would think that indisputable data and objective analysis would carry the day, ideas promoted by the expendable class invariably get rejected in lieu of ideas that come from entitled employees. As we have shown, the perspectives of nearly all long-term Intel employees (including that of Paul Otellini, who "grew up" at Intel) have been shaped in an environment where monopoly profits have masked problems. Consequently, they are less likely to see this dysfunctional pattern of decision making within the Intel bureaucracy, while it's all too

---

[103] "Boss Talk: Rewiring Intel; Addressing Past Glitches, CEO-to-Be Paul Otellini Sees Future in New 'Platforms'," *Wall Street Journal* (Eastern edition). New York, N.Y.: Jan 12, 2005. p. B.1.

clear to the more objective eye. Mentally, Grove Survivors are still grounded in the egalitarian foundation established by Bob Noyce, because amongst themselves (in the entitled class), things are still fairly equable. However, they fail to realize that since the days of Noyce, Intel has undergone subtle cultural changes, resulting in a deeply embedded class structure that has effectively destroyed the substance of egalitarianism. This reality can cause great frustration among the newer "world beater" employees within the expendable class, who hear the talk of an egalitarian culture but observe behaviors that are just the opposite.

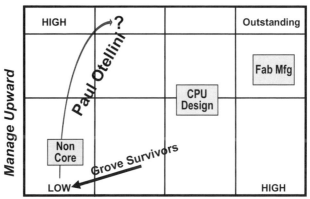

*Ability to Implement Change & Get Results*

# The Era of Denial

Such frustrated employees are probably unaware that, in the current (Paul Otellini) era, as in the recent past, the need for technical competence has been supplanted by the ability to present fancy foils in PowerPoint and manage upward, as depicted in the graphic above. The trends in implementing change and getting results, therefore, still mirror those of the Barrett era (a significant dropping off following the Grove era) after the rubber band was released.

The fallout from management inaction in the face of reality is profoundly pernicious and can be illustrated in the following simple example involving a manager and a rank-and-file employee. The employee was recently told by the manager that "It's not your job to object [to a given program proposal]. It's your job to make it work [by brute force]." [104] It must be emphasized that this case does not involve a

---

[104] Employee name withheld to preserve confidentiality.

lazy, "nay-saying" employee. To the contrary, this conscientious employee is quite aggressive and accomplished, having spent several years immersed in the details of success and failure, enough to gauge whether something will or will not work. In this particular case, the manager—who neither knows nor wants to know the details—was telling the employee to support a proposed approach that had been tried and had failed on three previous occasions (by the same personnel, by the way). Note that this is not an isolated case, but is quite common within many functional areas of Intel.

This example typifies the Intel culture where lower-level personnel are unable to expose realities and have them properly addressed. While the published Intel Values espouse "constructive confrontation" and "challenging the status quo," the actions of the entitled class suppress the exercise of these noble ideals such that, in practice, they are largely defunct. Interestingly, in his book *Confronting Reality*, Larry Bossidy has described several types of denial of reality, including "filtered information," which is manifest at Intel in the way that senior managers surround themselves with subordinates who always agree with them (or perhaps they have selective hearing); "wishful thinking," which corresponds to senior managers' insistence on seeing the world the way they'd like it, not as it truly is; and finally, denial of reality due to "fear."[105] The last type is the most disconcerting, as it seems to be the most common type of denial within Intel's senior management ranks.

Simply put, many senior managers don't know what to do about the reality, so they delegate it, hoping it will go away or be taken care of by subordinates. Some do just "the right amount of nothing" so as not to attract attention or be put at risk of failing (if they aren't good enough at "spinning" to escape accountability for failure). For example, a project manager explained what happened when his product development team was at a critical juncture, where future development would have to branch off in one direction or another. Each direction meant that a different large customer would not be well supported. The project manager brought all the data and analysis to his superiors, seeking unequivocal direction. Given the magnitude of this decision, it was incumbent on the senior managers to make the tough call and set

---

[105] Larry Bossidy and Ram Charan, *Confronting Reality: Doing What Matters to Get Things Right*, Crown Business, 2004

direction. However, the response to the project manager was a timid, "you decide, because we don't want to." The project manager was disappointed and rightly wondered what "value added" his superiors bring.[106]

In early 2005, Craig Barrett stated that the corporate cultural ills of 2004 had been reversed, citing Intel's improved financial performance in the last half of 2004 as proof. Many employees would disagree, yet hope that Paul Otellini's ascension to CEO will bring a revitalization of the Intel culture. Unfortunately for Intel, as "world beater" personnel come to understand the hopelessness of working within the Intel bureaucracy, they invariably leave the company for environments where their talents will be better utilized and appreciated, and this kind of exodus hurts Intel's ability to sustain operational performance over the long term.

## Business Process Fragmentation – Fallout from Denial

The authors of *Improving Performance: How to Manage the White Space on the Organization Chart* identify two forms of fragmentation in organizations: physical and cultural.[107] Physical fragmentation of processes is caused by the spatial separation of functions in any organization. The consequence of this separation is the time it takes for a transaction or process to travel from one organization to another—time usually wasted or non-value-added. Managers at many companies believe that they can get more results by adding more headcount in functional areas, but there has been no evidence to suggest that this practice is effective. As companies add more headcount in functional areas, they must also add more headcount to manage and coordinate the activities in the "white space" between those functions. This is how bureaucracies are formed. Intel has elevated this practice to an art form.

The second type of fragmentation is cultural, a form which is less obvious but the more serious of the two. It stems from a lack of alignment on priorities, which may be exacerbated by functionally focused metrics. Items that are a top priority for one group may be at the bottom for another. This also would hold true for departments and individuals, especially when different agendas and priorities vie for

---

[106] Employee wishes to remain anonymous
[107] Geary A. Rummler and Alan P. Brache, *Improving Performance: How to Manage the White Space in the Organization Chart*, Jossey-Bass, 1995

management attention. If you take a bureaucracy formed to manage white space as a culture that develops its own priorities (that may or may not be in agreement with functional areas), you end up with two types of intermediaries: operational and project-based. The operational intermediaries are required to keep the wheels on the car, whereas the project-based intermediaries are working toward landing the next big program. Sometimes these intermediaries are in conflict with one another because the project-based intermediaries are driving different agendas and priorities (which, as we have seen, may be ones that benefit their own career trajectories rather than the operations that they are supposed to be serving).

When you look at Intel with its different "classes" of people, some that are "entitled" and others "expendable," you see the depths of its cultural fragmentation. Couple Intel's cultural and physical fragmentation with the ambiguous corporate strategy and priorities typical of the Barrett era, and you have the makings of execution blunders such as the product roadmap mishaps and the cancellation in 2004 of liquid-crystal-on-silicon (LCOS) projects supporting Intel's planned entry into the consumer electronics market. Cultural fragmentation is evident in an environment where the entitled class manages upward to preserve or enhance status, and the expendable class tries to elevate operating realities in order to get systemic fixes to the rampant physical fragmentation; all the while, senior management remains oblivious to the execution challenges because the upward-managing layer filters out the bad news coming from below. By the time the problems become so large that entitled middle and senior managers can no longer ignore them, it is either too late to take corrective action (salvage the program) or management simply increases headcount, causing more fragmentation, patched with more human glue, to support operations. The increases in headcount and their effect on Intel's operational performance have become predictable: perhaps it is enough to say that Intel hired almost 20,000 people between the fourth quarter of 2005 and the first quarter of 2006.

When Intel's largely unrecognized fragmentation crisis is observed and understood, it becomes clear why the acquisitions made during the Barrett era never achieved the predicted growth and profitability announced to Wall Street. Chieftains of the various product divisions wanted to fund their programs without any real focus on the few products that would win in the competitive acquisition markets. The portfolio of products that were funded put such a burden on the manufacturing and supply chain infrastructure that it impeded several critical criteria for competing in those markets, notably time-to-market.

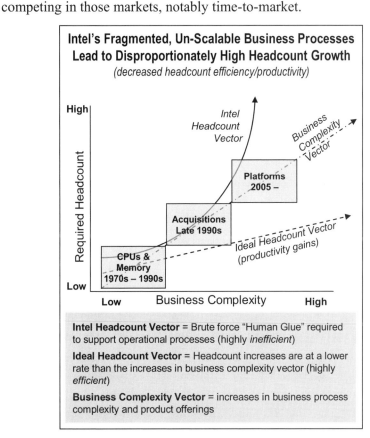

Unfortunately, Intel's microprocessor-producing machine was not geared to manufacturing high-mix low-volume products like those in the networking area, nor was it geared for the high-mix, high-volume communications market. Intel has yet to prove that it can turn on a dime inside its fab manufacturing environment. It takes 18 to 24 months to build and tool a new fab for microprocessor production. It's unknown how long it would have taken to convert a fab to support the newer products in the markets in which Intel intended to compete with its acquisitions. Beyond the question of fab agility, another overarching and unresolved issue is Intel's inability to thoroughly integrate its fab manufacturing with its Assembly and Test manufacturing into a seamless, highly responsive supply network.

A look at Intel's supply chain planning world provides further insight into the degree of fragmentation that exists at Intel. As stated earlier, the data regarding supply chain planning performance are alarming; suffice it to say that key indicators regarding Intel's supply chain agility show performance levels that are three to ten times worse than the industry standard—slower, more costly, more headcount required to execute, more homegrown applications needed, etc. The numbers clearly point to astronomical levels of physical fragmentation within Intel.

Fragmentation exists not only within the supply chain planning organization, but is also prevalent throughout much of Intel. Just as Intel's microprocessor-based competitive advantage has been far more potent than that of nearly any other company, so too has the fragmentation of its ancillary business processes and information systems been of stunning magnitude. The strength of Intel's core competency— its resultant cost and performance advantages flowing from its transistor-per-die, die-per-wafer, and capacity leadership—has, in essence, made it possible for Intel to achieve exceptional financial success in its CPU business, despite its monumental physical and cultural fragmentation. Unfortunately, the mismatch between Intel's core competency and the criteria for success with the acquisitions has left Intel no way to overcome its fragmentation and avoid a financial flop in the acquired business segments. This fragmentation potentially portends failure in the platform strategy because of the tremendous amount of coordination required to manage the "bundled" die in a platform (CPU, chipset, etc.) across not only the internal business units, but also those of external partners across Intel's global value chain.

The issue of fragmentation is very much related to that of employee differentiation. One of the purposes of embarking on the fragmentation discussion above was to further substantiate the claim that many managers within Intel's bureaucracy are, frankly, the wrong people for the job and should be replaced. Most managers who preside over Intel's fragmented business processes and information systems are individuals who grew up at Intel during the Grove boom years, in parallel with the growth of Intel's physical fragmentation. They have had *ample* opportunity during the Barrett era (years of slower growth, prodigious program funding, etc.) to streamline operations and eliminate this fragmentation, but have not been able to do so, let alone clearly articulate the problems. Instead, their grounding in and support of Intel's cultural fragmentation prevents them from giving credence to new individuals and information that would prove useful in meeting these challenges. The history of Intel's fragmentation makes it clear that the entitled or protected individuals within the mammoth bureaucracy, who retain or enhance their power by gaming the system and shutting out any hope of change, are without question the least equipped of Intel's employees to lead any attempted company transformation to build more integrated, efficient business processes.

## Technology and the "BAP"

> Remember your sacred responsibility to disappoint. That unsettling hunch you've got, now that the fuzzy front-end conversations are winding down, that the project will take longer than originally foreseen and will cost a lot more. Only by disappointing the project champion with this news in the beginning can you delight him in the end. Otherwise you end up being a slave to his unrealistic expectations, and instead of guaranteeing success, you're almost certain to produce failure.[108]
>
> David Schmaltz

It was 1998 and the Internet hype was reaching a fever pitch, yet Intel had not made any public statements about its ability to "eat its own dog food" and showcase Intel architecture as the backbone of the Intel e-commerce capability. Andy Grove went to his director of Internet Marketing and e-Commerce and stated that he wanted Intel to be able to take $1 billion in orders over the Internet within six months. This was a prime directive from the CEO, with the corresponding visibility and tension to motivate anyone.

Andy probably didn't have a good sense of what was truly required for this undertaking if it was going to be sustainable and, more importantly, drive further efficiency and productivity. Intel had already over-customized the Sales and Distribution module of its enterprise resource planning (ERP) system to the point that the ERP software company would no longer support it.

---

[108] *The Blind Man and the Elephant: Mastering Project Work, How to Transform Fuzzy Responsibilities Into Meaningful Results*, Berrett-Koehler Publishers, 2003

To meet the requested deliverable, the IT organization would essentially have to create a web front-end into the ERP in order to log the sales orders. It would require a lot of resources and money to accomplish this within six months. Moreover, in order to gain the efficiencies and productivity that the Internet economy purported to bring, a high degree of business process and system integration would be required. Unfortunately, the project team did not have enough time to do the things that would be sustainable while concurrently generating the efficiency and productivity desired. In essence, the project team worked its best magic under the "fire drill" circumstances to deliver the absolute bare minimum required to allow a customer to key in a sales order on the Intel website, but could not do the corresponding automation of the business processes to fulfill that order. What was actually delivered could be equated to a stage set built for a theatrical play. It looked good on the outside (web front-end), but when you opened the door, there was really nothing behind it (no integration to fulfillment). In essence, customers would key in their order and still have to call up an Intel customer service representative to secure supply commitments and delivery dates.

The website was implemented and Intel logged over $1 billion in sales orders over the six months, just as Andy had demanded. The website was viewed internally as a huge success. The marketing hoopla around this event is well known, and today over $20 billion a year in orders are taken over the website. The team that put the web order management tool in place worked very hard and admittedly cut a lot of corners in order to hit Andy's deadline. What's not known is that even though Andy's expected outcome was achieved, it was not a robust or sustainable solution that could provide the "Internet efficiencies" and business process improvements that generate productivity gains. Moreover, there was no longer any visibility to be gained by improving the web order management tool, which had been "good enough" to achieve Andy's desired *result*. This was a classic case of delegation to achieve "results at all costs" without consideration for long-term competitive advantage; where an inappropriate interpretation of Intel's value of "results orientation" completely trumped the sustainability focus of "process orientation" and the Intel Value of "doing the right things right." Despite this celebrated "result," Intel's process for committing supply to customers remained unimproved: Intel just inserted web-based technology into a process that was, and still is, highly manual. However, the director of Internet Marketing and e-Commerce who led this BAP or "big ass program" to completion was promoted to vice president and given the position of (joint) chief information officer (co-CIO), despite being eminently unqualified for the job. Once this particular fire drill was over, Andy moved his attention on to something else.

This story highlights two peculiarities that exist within the Intel culture. First is the belief that you can apply technology to solve problems without first gaining an understanding of the business process and root causes of those problems—which quite often have little to do with a lack of technology. In essence, technology is viewed as a panacea. The second peculiarity highlights Intel's penchant for large technical programs that promise revolutionary change and process improvement, but that create an environment where employees try to outdo each other as they come up with and sell to management those "BAPs" that will turbo-charge their career trajectories.

Without a doubt, Intel has skillfully employed its manufacturing technology to deliver high-quality products in high volumes at the lowest cost in the industry. The resulting high margins from this core competency have supported prodigious funding for other operational endeavors that aim to improve the more elusive measures of quality, such as on-time product delivery, supply flexibility, and responsiveness to customer inquiries. Unfortunately, it's in these areas that technology is too often viewed as *the answer* to rather than *the enabler* of business process change. Indeed, many of these Intel divisions have merely lived off of the success generated by Intel's renowned capability in fab process technology development instead of applying BKMs, where appropriate, to the circumstances in their respective functional areas. In essence, the profit engine of Intel's core competencies is funding many "BAPs" that don't contribute to Intel's bottom line. Although the people doing these BAPs would argue that they are adding business value, they have no way of measuring the actual results once the programs are delivered (if they're delivered at all): program managers do "back of the envelope" estimates of the return on investment (ROIs) to get programs justified and funded, but when the programs get delivered, no one measures to see if the results were actually achieved or whether they are sustainable.

During Intel's entrepreneurial era and throughout the boom years of the 1990s, Intel's engineering culture and its fragmented, ad hoc business process environment resulted in a dysfunctional combination that led to the creation of countless homegrown business applications. Driven by the "quick fix" mentality and the availability of generous funding, many "end-user software development" groups sprang up throughout the company and provided their customers with a myriad of point solutions that were needed merely to "keep the wheels on the bus" during Intel's high-growth years. These groups were generally small, agile, and customer focused, but they also led to an explosion of homegrown point solutions. Intel can't be completely faulted or criticized for this outcome because, at a macro level, the company was wildly successful. The development and use of these homegrown applications was actually pretty consistent with a common practice that says technology outside a company's core competency need not be world class or even on a par with similar technologies employed by the competition. Yet, the existence of these homegrown applications reveals a lack of competence, foresight, and leadership on the part of those who were stewards of the business processes at this time. Functional managers looked to optimize the processes directly under their control, rather than look to implement scalable solutions across connecting organizations to optimize the value chain. Each new point solution added to the growing web of fragmented applications, perpetuating and reinforcing the inefficient business processes in such a way that Intel's overall competitive position in non-CPU markets was impaired. It didn't matter in the CPU market segment because Intel's 80% share of it masked the need for efficiency; therefore, no credible effort was made to improve customer service. In non-CPU markets, Intel compensated by adding headcount to bridge the inefficiencies that were funded by the CPU cash cow.

By the late 1990s, things had changed a bit and many senior managers and personnel in the IT group began to realize that Intel could not be the best at developing custom software solutions that supported standard business processes. With this change in attitude came an increased faith and confidence in packaged software solutions…well, almost. Intel did start to implement various ERP modules in the mid 1990s, but they were riddled with countless customizations—ostensibly required to meet the needs of Intel's "different" environments. Furthermore, they were not delivering the business value that everyone had anticipated. By 2000, a strong anti-customization sentiment had gained momentum, such that senior IT managers talked about implementing new packaged software solutions in their "vanilla" state. They would insist that "the business processes will just have to be re-engineered in order to conform to the best-in-class business processes that are supported by these off-the-shelf solutions." Indeed, for many personnel, the pendulum had swung from "homegrown everything" to "absolutely no customizations!" This led to a new wave of BAPs and program managers looking to position themselves for career trajectory.

Toward the middle of 2000, the "no customizations" mantra caught the imagination of the newly appointed co-CIO who, after tackling the web order management challenge, was eager to transform all business processes that made use of information technology. This leader, full of bravado and backed by Intel's executive staff, made an aggressive assault on Intel's disastrous supply chain planning world by proposing several BAPs that would "clean up the mess." The mantra of the co-CIO became "overwhelm [programs] with resources" in order to "speed the change." This mantra was a consistent Intel approach whereby more headcount meant "we can go faster." The perceived value of such programs—staffed by dozens and sometimes *hundreds* of personnel—was primarily measured by the number of users or tools implemented, rather than by actual operational improvements enabled by the technology. While you can't fault the co-CIO's willingness to take risks (an Intel Value), these were not very informed risks, as Intel hastily spent enormous sums of money on software before it adequately understood the *extreme* challenges it faced with fixing the supply chain planning problems—data integration, business process re-engineering, user needs, and many other fundamentals. In fact, giddy IT personnel spent their time "playing" with the latest and greatest packaged software, eagerly looking for ways to just "throw it in" without achieving an adequate understanding of how it could be implemented to make processes more efficient and people more productive. Multiple iterations of software implementations ensued; none of them led to process optimization, but only created a black hole that devoured unthinkable amounts of financial resources and time. Unfortunately, none of the functional senior managers understood that implementing software "out of the box" meant that they had to change their business processes to fit the software. This would require changes that most of them were unwilling to make.

After a year or so it became apparent that many of these large programs were in such serious trouble that they could not be implemented without some fundamental changes. These programs became "technical white elephants,"[109] incremental monsters that were by-products of internal miscalculations facilitated by dysfunctional internal business processes. The conventional wisdom now shifted away from "implement 'vanilla' best-of-breed software solutions" to "first design the business processes" before turning to software. "Rules before tools" became the new mantra, where rules were derived from a clear understanding of the desired or "to-be" business process. For a while the IT folks sat on their hands while the more business-minded individuals participated in months-long design sessions creating elaborate, multi-level, soon-to-be business process designs. Oddly, despite these gloriously re-engineered designs, the IT program teams reverted to the "software as panacea" mentality, making only modest changes to the "big bang" implementation approaches previously attempted.

Intel's supply chain planning mess and the work of the program teams presents a scene much like the one described in Humpty-Dumpty: "all the king's horses and all the king's men, couldn't put Humpty together again." Instead of being able to land new solutions and accomplish the stated goal of improving the performance of supply planning operations by replacing many of the outdated, homegrown systems with new integrated systems, the repeated failures of the so-called business process and system experts just added more frustration to the user communities who were eager to see real improvements. In fact, in the outlying factory sites, end-user software teams started to spring up again (they had been highly discouraged by the new co-CIO), resuming the work of meeting users' immediate needs and adding to the web of homegrown applications. On the rare occasion that the IT group was able to land a new solution, it wouldn't replace or end the life of homegrown tools. By not doing this, IT added more complexity to the existing rat's nest of fragmented applications and prevented real business process change by giving people the option to revert to their old tools and business processes. Indeed, it would be an interesting exercise to compare Intel's multiple-system silos with those of IBM in the early 1990s. Lou

---

[109] "Your TWE Pocket Field Guide," Dave Molta, *Network Computing*, 4/1/2006

Gerstner, in his book *Who Says Elephants Can't Dance*, explains that "When I'd arrived at IBM, I wasn't taking too much for granted, but I did expect I'd find the best internal IT systems in the world. This might have been my greatest shock. We were spending $4 billion a year on this line item alone, *yet we didn't have the basic information we needed to run our business.* The systems were antiquated and didn't communicate with one another."[110] Gerstner's comments regarding IBM's IT systems ring true to Intel's current IT environment, with excessive headcount and countless spreadsheets making up the difference.

In many ways, Intel's desire and efforts to use the latest and greatest information technology could be compared to a hypothetical situation in which a novice financial planner attempts to sell his many investment products to a homeless person. The financial planner, so engrossed with all of the interesting and exciting investment vehicles at his disposal, is completely blind to the most pressing needs of the homeless—food, shelter, improved hygiene, clean clothing, opportunity, and skills—which are prerequisite to getting a job, let alone investing for the future or retirement.

When it comes to basic business processes across its value chain, Intel is not much different from this homeless person. Each year the entitled strategists hold "summit" meetings with senior managers and sell them on all the important "vehicles" going into the company's "capability roadmap" for the coming few years. They spew idiosyncratic platitudes and buzzwords pertaining to all the latest product development and supply chain information technology that will transform business processes. Year after year a similar "roadmap" is developed, and year after year, very little tangible progress is made toward achieving the main milestones on that roadmap. Accountability for real operational results is shockingly absent. Neither the IT nor the functional managers take on the responsibility or accountability for making the changes needed to achieve the operational improvements.

Again, this scenario leads back to Intel's fragmentation, which has proven to be an insurmountable stumbling block for many of Intel's business processes. Confidentiality prevents us from revealing how inordinate is the amount of human intervention and coordination required

---

[110] Lou Gerstner, *Who Says Elephants Can't Dance?* (New York, NY: HarperCollins, 2002), 65.

within Intel's value chain to run the business, as each functional area can have a plethora of disparate systems and data standards that are not integrated across the value chain. However, the numbers would be consistent with those of any company (in any industry) that has gone through rapid revenue and headcount growth similar to Intel's.

The concept and use of a true ERP system (integrated visibility of supply and demand throughout the internal supply chain) is foreign to the people in the operational environment. Without having these basics in place—like food, shelter, and other basics for the homeless person—all the smart-talk discussions of strategic capabilities never come to fruition. And if someone in attendance at a summit happens to have the intelligence, courage, and integrity to bring up the fundamental gaps in the basics, the discussion will invariably revert to the more "strategic" capabilities because "impending business conditions make it impossible to take the time that would be required to properly address the fundamentals…we need the strategic capabilities ASAP in order to compete." These "strategic capabilities" are pursued with BAPs that include large software investments. They inevitably fail. And the reason they fail is that focusing on the basics doesn't fit with the paranoia or the personal agendas of those who propose BAPs filled with sexy strategic stuff; management can't muster the organizational will or discipline to attack the difficult work of fixing the basics in an incremental fashion.

Despite the ups and downs experienced by the main IT organization, there is still a strong contingent of software program teams that have enough power to propose, year after year, large "strategic capability" programs where only the program names change. These teams are like guerillas in that they want to quickly attack a problem or implement solutions and then "grab the glory and run" before the customers are any wiser to the un-scalable nature of the solutions just implemented (that is, if the programs even reach implementation). It's actually become such a comedy that recently, Intel's ERP upgrade was renamed the "Enterprise Re-Platformization" program, to be more congruous to the latest platform strategy for Intel (this was clearly the quintessential symbol of managing upward!). The IT group has yet to demonstrate how the ERP software upgrade is going to enable Intel to drive growth in the new markets outlined by the new platform strategy. In fact, one factory planning manager summed it up appropriately by saying, "ERP hasn't done shit for us." (Anyone outside Intel who reads IT magazines will be surprised with this comment, given the ERP vendor's numerous print ads that tout the use of their software solutions to help make Intel "one of the best run companies in the world."). Internally, it clearly has become a culture of marketing and spinning.

The long-standing gaps that still exist with Intel's limited use of ERP capabilities will be exacerbated with the advent of the platform strategy, when bills of material, new product development and production coordination requirements become much more complex and challenging than ever before. Since the system and data basics are not in place, Intel will default to its modus operandi of adding more headcount in order to develop, manufacture, and ship platforms. History has shown that this "human glue" has only increased cycle times, exposing the lack of flexibility and agility that will further impede Intel's ability to effectively compete in an increasingly difficult marketplace. At the same time, the technology enthusiasts and strategists will become an even greater burden—not a benefit—to the operations "grunts" trying to execute to the platforms strategy, as the former try to land their fancy information system technologies on top of Intel's systems—and data—"house of cards." But since the functional managers have abdicated their ownership of business process improvements, they blindly follow the "experts" who promise to land BAP after BAP to catalyze the transformation of Intel's inefficient business processes.

The "quick fix" culture of Intel has repeatedly put its faith in BAPs and the long-tenured "heroes" who use technology as a crutch for solving every business process problem (to the point that it's technology for technology's sake), and hope at the same time that Intel can somehow leverage its own use of server hardware and fancy software to convince customers to buy more Intel silicon. Outside of Intel's core competency, the culture has looked at the use of technology as a panacea—an originator of momentum. Unfortunately, that momentum has proven to be sluggish, at best.

## Lessons Not Learned

There's a chronic, ongoing problem that has not been widely acknowledged or understood within Intel. One would think that it's a problem of customer-focused supply chain agility—and that clearly is one of the problems. But it's something more systemic: Intel senior management lacks an in-depth understanding of what supply chain management really means, how important it is when connecting to customers, and more specifically, how to fix this vexing problem. Over the years, there have been many attempts to fix Intel's supply chain planning and order fulfillment processes.

How bad is Intel's supply chain planning process? Just ask Intel's customers. In mid 2004, one of Intel's top three customers sent Craig Barrett a scathing, six-page letter that angrily complained about how difficult it is to do business with Intel, especially when it comes to getting timely and accurate delivery commitments to their changes in product orders. One very senior supply chain consultant with ties to a majority of the semiconductor industry's leading companies stated that "supply chain planners and planning organizations within the semiconductor industry are the very best of any industry…except at Intel, where they are, without a doubt, the very worst."[111]

As we have suggested (without divulging specific data points), key indicators of Intel's supply chain agility show performance levels that are three to ten times worse than the industry standard. These indicators include the cycle time to re-plan production schedules, respond to customer supply inquiries, and commit to delivery dates on customer orders; also included is the lack of a formalized process for statistically based demand forecasting. This range of performance also pertains to supply chain planner productivity and attrition rates, forecast accuracy, the size of teams working on supply chain software implementations, and the length of time to implement software. For the authors, these data points were hard to believe, indicating as they did that the world's largest semiconductor manufacturer wasn't a paragon of supply chain excellence.

There were several conclusions that could be drawn. On the obvious side, Intel compensates for its supply chain shortcomings by carrying high levels of inventory to meet customer demand. This is a worthwhile strategy: many semiconductor manufacturers make to stock, given the long fabrication lead times. However, another possibility is that, because Intel has had a virtual monopoly (~80% market segment share in microprocessors), there are very few occasions when high inventory

---

[111] Name and company withheld.

levels are problematic, except when there is a market softening or slowdown. Historically, the practice of "burning off" inventory has been perfected, whereby it usually takes only a quarter or so to whittle down the inventory levels before Wall Street gets nervous on the stock. Carrying high inventory levels affords Intel the luxury of leveraging third-party logistics firms and a worldwide logistics network to meet on-time delivery dates, which more than offset Intel's slow response time to supply commitment. It's not a bad balance—take longer to commit supply, but once you commit, stick to the delivery dates. Were it not for Intel's significant cost advantage—hence lower carrying costs—in fab manufacturing (derived from its transistor-per-die and die-per-wafer leadership), you would have to wonder how long the supply chain organization could stay in business. (Of course the market dominance in microprocessors doesn't hurt either).

Over the last twelve years, there have been at least eight attempts to improve the supply chain planning business processes, all of which have failed. Much of the churn in transforming the supply chain areas can be traced back to three fundamental weaknesses. The first is that program personnel lack the technical knowledge to implement process improvements, and compensate for this by ignoring planning users, preferring to make a "technology" implementation. The second weakness is that, since the planning personnel don't have the time or the technical competence to improve their own processes, they burn out very quickly, and excessive turnover is the result. A major difference between the supply chain program personnel and those in the trenches is the turnover rate. The third weakness is the functional area managers' lack of leadership and accountability. Functional and program leaders in this domain have an extremely low turnover rate, but a high rate of failure. Despite their repeated failures over 12 years and the hundreds of millions of dollars wasted, these Intel veterans smart talk their way to new rounds of funding while avoiding the real work of solving the systemic problems. Again, typically, they aren't held accountable for failure to improve processes and the hellish work life for rank-and-file planning personnel. As usual, employees find it disconcerting that most of the senior leaders who attempted improvements left the company after failing under Andy Grove's tenure, while those whose attempts failed under Barrett and Otellini still remain. To an outsider, this situation likewise seems unacceptable, not just because the amount of money spent on supply chain endeavors reaches into the tens of millions, but because the attempts have failed more than three times. One would think that someone in senior management would recommend that external consultants be brought in to lead the efforts successfully, rather than fund yet another set of Grove Survivors to attempt and ultimately fail.

The supply chain agility problems become more evident when you examine the characteristics of the non-CPU (personal computer) markets and Intel's inability to generate profitable growth over the last five years from communications and networking businesses. The lack of a track record in these markets, coupled with a much slower time-to-market, has hindered Intel's ability to make any kind of market share inroads. When your competitors can launch products within six months, but you are doing it in twelve, many market and revenue opportunities are lost— forever. This is just another symptom of the supply chain agility problem, which is a manifestation of Intel's larger problem, "corporate cholesterol,"[112] which produces business process inefficiencies and clogs the arteries of agility and innovation, making it difficult for the company to compete.

Even if Intel were to move into manufacturing communications and networking silicon internally, its supply chain problems would still exist. The basis of competition in these newer markets (and Intel's market position) is radically different than in microprocessors, especially when it comes to customer service levels, product-mix changes, gross margin, and cost competitiveness. Another competitive factor is time-to-market: communications and networking product lifecycles are changing more rapidly than in the microprocessor markets. Interestingly, Intel indirectly controlled time-to-market early in the microprocessor era until IBM and AMD became formidable players and challenged the 18-month product lifecycle. However, it appears to the authors that Intel lacks the robust processes in product development lifecycle management to truly compete in these newer communications and networking markets. Moreover, the company lacks the supply chain expertise needed to integrate product development lifecycles into its manufacturing and planning arenas, especially outside of microprocessor markets. Even within microprocessor markets, as we have seen, Intel's supply chain

---

[112] *Business Integration Journal*, February 2005, 27.

responsiveness is woefully below industry benchmarks, so Intel compensates by using its high manufacturing capacity muscle and carrying high levels of inventory to meet the required customer service levels.

The discovery of these product development and supply chain problems leaves one to ask how these things could go on at Intel without management scrutiny and subsequent action to fix them. If the "virtual monopoly" answer seems oversimplified, another plausible answer, until recently, has been that Intel's growing profitability covered a multitude of sins. During the Andy Grove era, Intel experienced an average annual growth rate of 40%, and this pattern continued into the early years of the Barrett era (for example, in 1999 the microprocessor business grew by 44%). In other words, as a rising tide lifts all boats, this booming growth rate masked product development and supply chain problems, all of which still exist to this day.

The growth of Intel during the 1990s resulted in repeated stock splits and gave Intel employees a tremendous sense of shared wealth, accomplishment, and satisfaction. Much of this pride was well deserved, because supporting the growth required enormous sacrifices throughout much of the company. (Intel is well known for driving employees to work long, hard hours.) However, the company's overall success also brought the pernicious side effects of increasing employee arrogance and reinforcing the already strong "not invented here" culture. This was especially deleterious among those employees and leaders in the non-core, under-performing product and functional areas like supply chain management and information technology, because it deluded them into thinking that they were best-in-class performers. Though nothing could be further from the truth, you can imagine that if the company is selling a lot of products, revenue has increased to record levels, and gross margins are healthy, no one is going to say there is something wrong with the company's supply chain management or time-to-market.

But the good times did not last forever. After the third quarter 2004 results were released to the public, at a time when Intel was experiencing its share of missteps, Craig Barrett told employees that Intel had always had its share of setbacks, but that in past years the problems were masked by a booming demand for PCs. He went on to say, "We're on the tail end of a recession, and the same sorts of product issues are viewed in an entirely different light. It's not an excuse—it's the reality of the situation."[113] Barrett's point was right in that it was not an excuse; however, the behaviors developed during the '90s boom years have continued to breed a culture of arrogance and resistance to change, where poor functional performance tends to be overlooked.

It is no surprise that many astute employees recognize that Intel lags the industry in supply chain responsiveness by a factor of 10, but in the microprocessor market this has not been an inhibiting factor, given Intel's market segment share. This poor performance, however, does have major implications for Intel in non-CPU (personal computer) markets. Addressing the perpetual supply chain integration problem is what Andy Grove would call a "strategic inflection point" that Intel needs to overcome in order to achieve supply chain parity and establish a competitive position in these markets, where they have little or no market share. Furthermore, by fixing its supply chain integration problem, Intel would offer evidence that it is successfully addressing its biggest overall cultural problem. Overcoming this problem would show that Intel is learning how to preserve and leverage its existing strengths while innovating and developing new core competencies that will lead the company into a new era of growth.

The supply chain problems are noteworthy because they illustrate the multitude of problems that arise directly and indirectly from the culture of entitlement at Intel. It has become evident that the biggest problem confronting the company is its inability to effectively inspect or enforce adherence to the published Intel Values. The lack of adherence to the Values would imply removing people (even from the company) when those Values are repeatedly violated, but as we have shown, senior management at Intel is either "out of touch" with reality or simply denies that there is something inherently wrong with the culture, even though it's impacting operational performance.

Most of Intel's expendable employees and a few entitled employees are aware of this problem, but they feel powerless to do anything about it. Whereas roughly half of Intel's employees have been with the company for fewer than five or six years, the overwhelming majority of middle and senior managers have been around for 15 to 20 years or more. It's many of the newer employees, especially those who have

---

[113] Intel Employee webcast, 2004, Intel Employee website.

gained wisdom and perspective from significant pre-Intel work experience, who can best discern Intel's cultural anomalies. They see that the management ranks are filled with people who, in the absence of clear or rigorous performance metrics, learned how to rise faster than the "rising tide" by exhibiting the behaviors discussed in previous chapters—getting results at all costs, building their networks or relationships, and being strategically servile with managers who reward sycophantic behavior. Unfortunately for Intel, the majority of these managers, having professionally grown up in-house, with little or no previous work experience, did not exhibit the right skill sets to successfully execute Intel's acquisition strategy. It would not be a stretch to postulate that they do not have the right skill sets to successfully lead the company through the platform strategy, either, with its many new challenges.

Finally, many of these individuals are "stuck" with having to work for a living (their stock options are under water[114]) and therefore they cling tenaciously to their positions. From the late 1990s into early 2000, many Intel managers and senior individual contributors would cavalierly joke about being able to "call in rich" at any time and retire on a moment's notice because their stock options were worth millions. That changed in the latter half of 2000 as Intel stock plummeted. Many of these option-rich employees did not cash in during the Internet bubble when they had a golden opportunity to do so; perhaps they were a bit greedy and believed the stock would go up indefinitely. If you talk with some of these employees they will tell you, "I used to come to work because *I liked to* work at Intel. Now I come to work because *I have to* work." Their net worth has dramatically decreased due to the lower stock price, making early retirement impossible. This is unfortunate for several reasons, but there is also the question whether other companies would pay them salaries anywhere near what they earn at Intel, or whether other companies would hire them in the first place.

The confluence of factors affecting these managers—their bonds with fellow "Grove Survivors" in the entitled class, their myopic view of reality based on Intel's profitable past, their regret for not cashing in when they had the chance, their deluded hope that the stock will rise

---

[114] When the actual stock price is lower than the strike price of the options – in other words, the stock options are worthless.

again, and their need to keep working—drives them to tenaciously protect their territory. Unlike the best leaders, who are usually unselfishly devoted to the good of the company, these individuals are perpetually concerned with personal gain, be it higher grade levels, more money, managing more headcount, or the *coup de grâce*, the coveted title of vice president. Of course, they give lip service to doing "what's right for Intel," but their actions tend to prove otherwise.

## A Letter to Paul Otellini

If objective outside observers, such as management consultants or a "Lou Gerstner" type, were to do a thorough assessment of Intel's competitiveness across product development, marketing, supply chain, and other areas, would Intel's senior management listen? More importantly, would Paul Otellini listen? Would any bold actions be taken? Maybe that would depend on the letter.

> To: Paul Otellini
> From: Managing Partner, High-Tech Consulting Firm
>
> Dear Paul:
>
> I know that when you and I first talked, you wanted me to do a thorough analysis of Intel's competitive position and future prospects for organic growth. You also wanted me to informally assess the morale of the rank-and-file employees, their understanding of the platform strategy, and their willingness to get behind it to make it a reality. As consultants, it is incumbent upon us to perform assessments such as these objectively, without regard for potential impact on future business with our firm. I do, however, hope that you will take our assessment seriously and consider extending the engagement, so we can assist Intel in addressing some of the opportunities uncovered. We conducted well over two thousand interviews with product design engineers, factory quality and reliability, factory planners and technicians, logistics, IT, purchasing, and program management personnel across all functional areas and business units.
>
> Upon extensive discussion with some of my colleagues at the firm on how best to approach communicating our assessment, it was felt that we would take a direct approach, utilizing one of your own Intel Values of being open and direct:
>
> Paul, WAKE UP! THE EMPOROR HAS NO CLOTHES! In my twenty-plus years in consulting, I would have never believed that a company that changed the world could let itself slip into the complacency I have witnessed! It's difficult for me to start in any particular area, so I'll to begin the assessment by addressing the

overarching issues and then narrow them down to the more specific ones.

First, we wanted to understand everyone's idea of a Platform Strategy. Obviously, having the website on the corporate intranet was a good grounding exercise; however, upon reviewing all the interview content, it is clear that there were relatively few, if any, instances where we were able to get a common answer from employees. Not only did we find different answers between groups, but different answers within groups. That wasn't as troubling, though, as people's not knowing how the work they were performing was contributing to any specific corporate objectives. People were just doing what their managers told them to do without questioning the validity of the work. The same finding occurred in the managers that we interviewed. More disturbing was that there weren't specific goals or targets that divisions were marching toward, or process metrics for tracking performance against those goals. It was also surprising to find that senior leaders were somewhat evasive in admitting accountability. We would get answers like, "I'm accountable for the launch of this product," but there was no revenue goal or market segment share goal they would admit to. It was as simple as once the product launched, they considered their result officially achieved, and their accountability no longer was required. Once we interviewed rank-and-file employees, there was even more ambiguity about what results were critical to corporate-level objectives. In some cases, it seemed like groups "made up" work that they thought would contribute to their group, but had no idea how it contributed to adding value for Intel as a whole. We received quite a few comments from people about making sure that they were working on something so that they had "accomplishments" for focal. Our interviews and observations demonstrated that the lower in the ranks we went, the more we witnessed disconnections between what people were working on and what we understood to be required for executing your Platform Strategy.

Paul, three things are clear: first, you have a huge disconnect between your strategy and the execution of that strategy among senior management and the rank and file. The level of understanding and the degree of coordination will not drive the level of performance that you are expecting. Second, there is a complete lack of accountability at the senior management level. Goals and objectives don't meet the SMART (Specific, Measurable, Achievable, Relevant, Time bound) criteria, making it plainly obvious that no one is on the hook for anything that can be measured. Another interesting finding from our consultants' observations, as well as feedback from your employees, is that senior managers aren't consistently demonstrating your Intel Values. We noticed that they discuss them a lot, but their actions consistently contradict them. There also seems to be a preoccupation with managing upward and self-advancement, but not much action on improving operational performance in their respective areas. Third, employee morale is absolutely terrible. There is a fear in the air that seems to be connected to focal. When we asked people about focal, we were able to glean some common themes. The first was that people felt the process was no longer objective, but that it seemed to be subjective, with outcomes that are easy to game. The second theme people expressed is that there was no longer a meritocracy based on results, but on popularity.

In the operational support areas, there are also some common themes. First, Intel has excessive headcount and division of labor that tops anything we've seen before. Jobs tend to be narrowly defined, and to put it bluntly, you have two or three people doing one person's job, especially in the management ranks. The two-in-a-box is overused, with no obvious purpose other than sticking two people together at the same grade level to share responsibilities. It seems every VP has a TA and every senior manager (non-VP) has the equivalent of an "operations manager." Your CIO role seems to be a revolving door for VPs rather than a corporate-level strategic position. We were trying to understand why you have over 200 VPs but only five Platform divisions and could not come up with an answer to justify having that many VPs with no P&L responsibility. In short, you have a disproportionately high number of generals. In the rank and file, we saw similar headcount and division of labor discrepancies. It also appears that you have duplicated the microprocessor headcount model in the non-microprocessor divisions. The headcount carried for microprocessor may be justified; however, it is not in those other divisions where margins are lower and agility is paramount. The excessive overhead is hurting profitability in those divisions and appears to have done so for the last four-to-five years, according to our analysis of your financials and the annual reports. It takes Intel two-to-three times longer than necessary to accomplish core activities like new product development, plan production or even respond to customers on simple supply inquiries. People are stepping over each other, most of them trying to reconcile data between groups. We also observed that there is poor, if any, coordination across functional groups, leaving people guessing on what needs to be accomplished. Your senior managers are very protective of their turf and seldom see the cross-functional connections required to meet customer objectives. The rank and file won't do any work that isn't sanctioned from above, and they are afraid to raise red flags to management for fear of retribution (focal).

Most of your product development is either done in a vacuum without regard for customer needs or is a direct reaction to your competitor's successful design strategies. There has been virtually no real innovation outside of your core microprocessor and fab technology development core competencies, yet you have spent and wasted billions on worthless acquisitions and a failed foray into online services—another $400 million dollar write-down. You have to ask yourself one question: "If you didn't have the virtual monopoly profits from microprocessors, would you do things differently?"

In summary, you are top heavy, bureaucratic, and inefficient across most, if not all the organizations. Employee morale is terrible, you're bleeding talent, and most of your senior management is "fat, dumb and happy" living in a world without accountability. The lack of senior management adherence to the Intel Values only adds fuel to the fire. Instead of hiring more headcount (as part of a growth strategy) with all of your microprocessor profits, increase the dividend. GET LEAN AND MEAN! It's time to clean house.

Sincerely,

Managing Partner, High-Tech Consulting Firm
P.S. Our firm is available to assist you in your next steps.

cc: Andy Grove

A few vital questions must be answered before Intel's future prospects can be determined. Will Paul Otellini be able to discern the harmful cultural patterns of behavior as he launches his bold new platform initiatives? Will he be able to recognize that destructive behaviors, which have historically hindered Intel's efforts to diversify outside of its core CPU business, must be corrected if his platforms strategy is to succeed? Moreover, will he see that these harmful behaviors have been eroding and will continue to erode the performance within Intel's areas of core competence? If he can ask and appropriately answer the questions above, will he then be able to come to the realization that the single biggest problem facing Intel is the impact of the culture on operational performance? Will he realize this is what has affected Intel's ability to execute? And will he realize that this need to clean house extends much deeper than merely having Barrett take care of his "dirty laundry" in Intel's upper ranks, as he did before handing over the CEO reins? Besides growing Intel revenue to $70 billion by 2009, what are the specific annual financial goals? Why hasn't Paul Otellini communicated them to all Intel employees? More importantly, why hasn't he assigned accountability for these goals? Finally, will Otellini be remembered for letting the Intel bureaucracy continue to grow and stymie execution, or will he establish a Jack Welch-like legacy for cleaning out Intel's bureaucracy and putting practices in place to keep it out?

## Evolution of Intel Culture

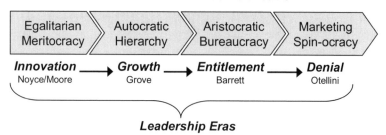

*Leadership Eras*

Otellini has the power to begin transforming the Intel culture so that it will directly or indirectly seek out, identify, and confront the ugly realities it now faces. Restoring confidence in the published Intel Values starts with properly addressing problems by inspecting for adherence to the published Values. Senior management should first start by cleaning up in its own ranks, making public examples of senior, long-time employees to let people know that Intel is serious. This has been proven in other Fortune 500 companies as a sure way to restore confidence in management and rank-and-file employees. Otellini should also look at eliminating the layers of middle management in grade levels 9 through 12, and narrow the distance between senior management and the realities of the rank and file. Although the authors believe that Paul Otellini persists in denial of these needs, time will tell whether he is, or is not, out of touch with his opportunities.

**VALUES SUMMARY**

Paul Otellini must address all the Intel Values; however, the ones that will require more attention are those that were lacking in the leadership actions of both Andy Grove and Craig Barrett:

**RISK TAKING**

⇒ Listen to all ideas and viewpoints

**GREAT PLACE TO WORK**

⇒ Work as a team with respect and trust for each other

**CUSTOMER ORIENTATION**

⇒ Listen and respond to our customers, suppliers and stakeholders
⇒ Deliver innovative and competitive products and services
⇒ Make it easy to work with us
⇒ Be vendor of choice

**BEHAVIOR SUMMARY**

The predominant behaviors of the Intel culture described in this chapter:

⇒ Not embracing change and challenging the status quo
⇒ Not constructively confronting and solving problems
⇒ Not acknowledging reality
⇒ Not managing performance objectively, fairly and firmly
⇒ Not holding senior managers to the same level of scrutiny as rank and file

# Chapter 9

# Employee Disengagement

> The dogmas of the quiet past are inadequate to the stormy present…As our case is new, so we must think anew, and act anew. We must disenthrall ourselves.
>
> Abraham Lincoln
> Annual message to Congress, Dec. 1, 1862

The lack of acknowledgement from Craig Barrett, Paul Otellini, and other senior managers that the culture is no longer vigorous, but cancerous, has led many people in both entitled and expendable classes to intellectually and emotionally disengage themselves from efforts to make a difference. Several dimensions of this employee disengagement require elaboration if readers are to truly understand the behaviors that oppose the establishment of any kind of momentum at Intel. There's an insider's perspective, which is based on the bond that ties together the Grove Survivors, who use the system they've become experts at gaming to preserve their positions. There is also an outsider's view, represented by newcomers to Intel who read the company Values and try to live them to the letter, only to encounter the opposing behavior of the insiders. The rest of this section will focus on an outsider's perspective.

An outsider, who may come from another company or industry, first experiences a metaphorical "cold slap in the face" while observing some of the attitudes and behaviors of Intel employees and recognizing the conspicuous lack of competence among many senior functional managers, especially in support groups to manufacturing. If you are one of the many Intel employees hired toward the end of, or after, the Grove era, and if you work in an under-performing area of the company, you must fight a daily battle to establish your credibility and retain your own sense of self-worth, especially if you were an experienced hire or brought in as part of an acquisition. Before joining Intel, you may or may not have realized that the dues you had paid and the credibility you had worked hard to establish would most certainly be worthless at Intel. Once you realize this fact, you still trudge along in the belief that, over time, you can make a positive difference in your organization, because that belief is fueled daily by your knowledge that the Intel organization to which you belong is grossly under-performing. In some areas, the performance is so sub-par that turning things around might take a long time and constitute a meaningful career's worth of work. You know the road will be bumpy, but you think that this once-in-a-lifetime opportunity to make a difference is too good to pass up, so you dig in.

In your naivety, you believe that the published Intel Values are consistent with employee behaviors, so you model your behavior accordingly by attacking the problems of poor functional performance, and you are careful not to attack the personnel who have been the stewards of this poor performance for years and years. You bring to bear all of your know-how by utilizing appropriate data, analysis, and the experience from your own successes and failures to support your approach to solving the problems. Even though your proposal is completely consistent with Intel Values (challenges the status quo, incorporates learning from successes and failures, pays attention to detail, is customer oriented, etc.), surprisingly, it is met with violent resistance. Shortly after you've shared your ideas, owners of the approach to previously failed solutions will step forward and offer a modified version of their failed solution. On the surface, this proposal will incorporate some of the benefits and language of *your* proposal, a sign that your message resonated and caught the attention of some key individuals, especially in the management ranks. However, after a closer examination you will see that the competing proposal, a modification of the previous failure, is fundamentally no different than what had been tried unsuccessfully before.

The two proposals are then discussed in various forums for a number of weeks or even months. Middle and senior managers from a number of affected functional areas and programs must be spun up on the new proposals before they can make a decision. In the industry outside of Intel, a typical senior manager within a particular domain would most likely be initiating this type of effort or at least have the ability and inclination to dig into the details of what is being proposed, so he or she could quickly discern a good proposal from a bad one. However, Intel is indeed different in this regard, so this education process will continue and eventually culminate in a meeting of 40 or more persons who are to debate the merits of the two proposals and reach a decision. But the debate rarely happens, because lower-level committees will have decided on a recommendation beforehand.

Unbeknownst to you, once the competing proposal emerged, your proposal was as good as dead. Why? Your proven track record and domain expertise were somehow unable to compete with the unbreakable Grove Survivor bond. It's that simple. It had nothing to do with the merits of your proposal or your ability to execute, but you didn't yet know this; it was your first time through this decision-making process. Come to think of it, maybe the outcome had *everything* to do with your proven track record and domain expertise and the merits of your proposal and your ability to execute. It may have been shot down because it would make the Grove Survivors look incompetent, since they hadn't come up with the idea themselves. A senior manager gave the following advice to one of the authors: "You have to make others believe that the proposal was their idea in order to sell it and make it successful." That advice from a superior, at a company that so proudly promotes "constructive confrontation" and "challenge the status quo"? It's no wonder that innovation at Intel is all but dead.

At this point, if you're patient, you *hope* that you can try again at some future point and be successful. You "disagree and commit," which is what Intel expects of you, even when you know that the decision made was wrong and will fail—not that you are "smarter" than anyone else, but you've done due diligence in your research, you're experienced, and you know the team contains and is being led by many individuals with a history of consistent failure. Furthermore, the program displays many of the characteristics that are found in BAPs. All the same, you don't wish misfortune on the team, so you move on to something else, divorcing yourself from the impending failure. The program goes forward with great fanfare but eventually ends up failing, or the schedule gets pushed out a time or two (or more) until the program finally capitulates and goes back to the drawing board. As pointed out by Tim Jackson, Intel can be tenacious in "persevering with a project long after it was proven a mistake,"[115] so it may take a very long time to reach the point of total capitulation. Once there, the cycle repeats itself. No lessons are ever learned from the mistakes, because admitting those would be admitting that the wrong decisions were made, and such admissions would reflect poorly on the people who made the decisions—usually senior managers. No one wants that kind of attention, because that would put a wrench in their performance review and make it difficult to continue gaming the focal system.

By this time, if you are not yet onto this game, and if you are striving to be a competent leader, you look in the mirror and ponder what things you could have done better to sell your idea. You review Steven Covey's *Seven Habits*[116] and you redouble your efforts to improve your "win-win" thinking, your building of relationships, your empathy, etc. You go back into the committee and pitch your proposal again, supported by your data and analysis, avoiding the temptation to carry an "I told you so" attitude. For a time you have a receptive audience because they are still stinging from the previous failure. But the listening ears are soon shut once the reality starts to set in and program leaders and committee members realize how long and difficult the road ahead will be to truly address and fix the systemic problems. At this point the architects of the previously failed solution emerge, this time with a "new and improved" program name and enough new material to convince everyone that this time will be different. You see this new competing proposal for what it is—a specious repackaging of the status quo—but you cannot get any of the incumbents to go along with you. You realize that your adherence to the *Seven Habits* doesn't matter any more than the Intel Values, because the culture of Intel is built on a reactive, quick-fix gestalt, held together by the Grove Survivor's bond. So you decide to find a different job in an interesting area within another functional group...only to experience more of the same.

Ultimately, you realize that Intel operates on a dysfunctional personnel management model. Despite Craig Barrett's statements to the contrary, the architects of costly repeated failures are *rarely* held accountable or

---

[115] Tim Jackson, *Inside Intel* (New York, NY: Penguin Group, 1997), 219.
[116] Steven Covey, *The Seven Habits of Highly Successful People* (Free Press, 15th Anniversary edition November 9, 2004)

moved to make way for non-entitled personnel to lead. Sadly, you realize that your once-in-a-lifetime opportunity to fix a broken functional area at Intel was really nothing more than a mirage that you had been chasing for quite some time. Once this reality sets in, you have no choice but to either compromise your integrity and start playing the game yourself (though you're at a big disadvantage because you are not a Grove Survivor), completely disengage, or sadly (for you and Intel), because you feel strongly that you could initiate meaningful change and improvement if given a fair opportunity, you leave Intel.

## Losing Faith in the Intel Values

The time has come to realize that the culture cannot heal itself when it is a culture of greed supported by incestuous relationships. The deep familial bonds among those who run Intel make it clear that it is time for an outsider to come in to clean house and reinvigorate the once-mighty culture of Intel. In *The 7 Hidden Reasons Employees Leave*, Leigh Branham compiled a list of 67 reasons employees leave companies, based on thousands of exit interviews completed by employees. As he grouped those reasons for leaving, his analysis culminated in a list of four common denominators.

1. The Need for Trust
2. The Need to Have Hope
3. The Need to Feel a Sense of Worth
4. The Need to Feel Competent[117]

Not surprisingly, our own observations and the information we've gained from informal interviews with countless employees are completely consistent with Branham's research. We will discuss Branham's four denominators in the context of Intel by starting with the first, the need for trust.

The need for trust seems quite simple on the surface; however, it has tremendous effects on employee morale. It has to do with an employee's expectation that management delivers on its promises; that they are honest, open and direct in all communications with employees; that they

---

[117] Leigh Branham, *The 7 Hidden Reasons Employees Leave: How to Recognize the Subtle Signs and Act Before It's Too Late* (New York, NY, AMACOM, 2005), 19-25.

invest in employees, treat them fairly, and compensate them fairly.[118] When management tells employees one thing and does another, or when management shares information with employees only after it's been made public (employees have learned about it first in the press), this kills trust in management. In a healthy environment, managers would communicate the good, the bad, and the ugly to employees in a timely manner—before such news becomes public. This would allow employees to assimilate the information and offer support and possibly ideas on how best to address problems or issues. Removing fear from the culture is a first step in the right direction. Employees fear speaking up because they don't trust management. Having worked at other large Fortune 500 companies, the authors can attest that when senior managers make themselves accessible, employee trust is assured. We have experienced it elsewhere.

The second is the need to have hope, which for employees is the belief that they will be able to grow, develop their skills on the job and through training, and have the opportunity for advancement or career progression leading to higher earnings.[119] Historically, when times get tough, the two expenditures that are first to go are travel and training expenses. This has been predictable ever since we can remember. It's understandable to cut travel expenses, but training is extremely important, especially if you are undertaking a new initiative and need the skills in order to be successful.

Two disturbing behavioral patterns have emerged at Intel over the last five or six years, both involving training. The first concerns managerial approvals of training. It takes a Herculean effort to get manager approval of training if classes run longer than one or two days. Forget that you need it to be successful in your job or that the training is in your individual development plan. Even managers don't have any real development training. Up until 2005, middle- and senior-management training was non-existent. Unless you were one of the privileged few that were sent to Stanford for eight weeks, there was nothing to prepare you for your functional area unless you took it upon yourself to seek training outside of the company. The second pattern is, in our humble opinion, more damaging than the first, but it too arises from management's lack of support for training. It is that most of the really good training requiring

---

[118] Ibid.
[119] Ibid.

as little as three, four, or five days has been shortened to one or two days. This has occurred because of managers' desire to keep their employees on the job more instead of in training classes. The undesirable outcome, however, is that the quality of training has declined to the point where most of it isn't worth taking; you don't learn anything. The only training that hasn't been affected by this pattern is in the area of fab manufacturing.

A third common denominator affecting peoples' desire to stay with (or leave) a company is the need to feel a sense of worth, which is akin to feeling confident that if you work hard, do your best, demonstrate commitment and make significant contributions, you will be recognized and rewarded accordingly.[120] Feeling worthy also means that you will be respected and regarded as a valued asset and not expendable to the company. It was made quite clear in earlier chapters that rank-and-file employees are considered expendable. What's not widely known is how many employees in those ranks are actually aware of this. Unfortunately, Intel has become quite hierarchical, and to make matters worse, not only has the focal system failed to weed out poorly performing managers, it has created so many two-in-a-box roles that the leadership pipeline is perpetually clogged to those with any talent reaching from below. There is no longer incentive to work hard and try to make significant contributions because there really isn't a reward worthy of your contributions. There aren't even any decent lateral positions, or if there are, the hiring manager opens up an external requisition that has qualifications on it that are far beyond the hiring manager's—which has never made any sense. Why would a person who is more qualified than the hiring manger accept a job that the hiring manager isn't even qualified to manage?

The fourth denominator is the need to feel competent, which is the expectation on the part of employees that they will be matched to a job that utilizes their talents, skills, and competencies; where the job is challenging, and they receive training (as needed) to perform the job capably; where they see the results of their work and obtain regular feedback on their performance.[121] At Intel, as we've shown, not only do employees have difficulty getting training, but constructive, regular

---

[120] Ibid.
[121] Ibid.

feedback and satisfaction from seeing the results of their work are elusive qualities as well, because most managers are detached from the day-to-day realities and details of the work. When an employee raises an issue, the manager often chooses not to "rock the boat" to his or her own manager (always chooses the status quo); some don't even respond to you when you disagree with them over a direction. Likewise, there are many examples at Intel of employees being poorly matched to their jobs, either because their talents aren't utilized or because they lack competence for the job they're assigned. As we have shown, this happens even at the highest levels of the company. Our primary example has been the supply chain, where senior executives spend 20 years in manufacturing and then get assigned to manage the supply chain, where they are literally fish out of water.

Now that the common denominators of employee disengagement have been discussed, it's time to highlight the anomalies that have caused employees to lose faith in the Intel Values. Employees have a few questions on their minds that senior management must answer. The first question is whether the current leadership can steer Intel to success.[122] Employees want to know whether their leaders have the right vision and strategy, the right people in the right positions, and the competence and strength of character to lead Intel into new markets and rekindle the growth that everyone expects from a high-technology company. Currently, confidence is lacking, given the senior management track record since the departure of Andy Grove.

A more important question is whether employees can trust senior management to do what they say.[123] In the Barrett era, certainly, managers verbally espoused the Intel Values, but little (if any) action backed up those words. More recently, Paul Otellini's words and actions have left something—much—to be desired. People disengage, for good reason, when they realize that their leaders say one thing but do another. What's worse is when leaders are not honest with their employees and try to hide their intentions. An extreme example was provided by senior leaders at Enron, who told employees that everything was looking bright and that they should buy the stock, while the leaders themselves were selling it off. Many of the long-tenured Grove Survivors have too much

---

[122] Ibid, 183-186.
[123] Ibid.

faith in their comrades because they grew up together and share 'familial' bonds, whether they are from stock appreciation or working together over the years. Their patience may be a virtue, but it also fosters angst. They are now waiting and waiting and waiting for that stock to appreciate so that they can cash out. Many of them are dead weight—they can't leave and can't retire.

The last question is whether senior management has trust and confidence in the employees. Employees know that senior management needs their commitment to make the platform strategy work. Unfortunately, most people don't understand or haven't been given to understand what it means to them, and senior management is so disconnected from the realities of the rank and file that they don't realize people are mostly disengaged. In fact, over the last two-to-three years, you can't imagine how many people have started their own initiatives outside of the company—selling real estate, teaching classes at the local university, starting their own home businesses—almost all of which has been done out of frustration and a lack of trust in senior management.

Over the course of the last five years a number of questions have surfaced amongst rank-and-file employees about what needs to change in the culture in order to bring it more in line with the published Intel Values. Although the solutions seem like basics that people outside Intel would assume to be practices and values already in place, they genuinely are not.

### 1.  Why is there a mismatch between authority and accountability?

Under Andy Grove, managers had the authority to make the necessary decisions to get things done and were accountable for the results of those decisions. Authority without accountability breeds mediocrity among managers and distrust among employees. Accountability without authority prevents managers (or others) from getting anything done efficiently and hurts Intel's operational performance. Employees are tired of seeing grade 12 senior managers who fail in one group get moved to head another. The cream doesn't rise to the top in this situation. Program managers who are accountable for results but have no authority to make critical operational decisions are set up to fail. A former senior manager summed it up well: "When someone sets up another person to fail so that they can succeed, the program or organization fails."[124]

Holding every employee to the same standards means equalizing the grade levels across groups and establishing criteria for moving from one level to another. Holding everyone accountable to the Intel Values means that *everyone* is measured on their adherence to the published Values, without exception. Senior managers and rank-and-file employees should be equally accountable to the Intel Values and the consequences for not adhering to them should be the same for all.

### 2.  *Where is the inspired leadership?*

Intel certainly isn't suffering for strategies; there are more strategies than implementations of those strategies. Leadership means choosing the right people for the right positions. Leaders must have those two qualities we described earlier in the book: technical competence and the ability to execute. These are the two key ingredients of any good leader, and they certainly were present during the Grove era.

Getting the right people into the right positions is the non-negotiable starting point. All other themes flow from taking care of this first and most important matter. Without this, there can be no true success at trying to implement the subsequent recommendations. Mr. Shareholder wanted to know who to fire, and this book has tried to clearly identify which employees within Intel should go.

Choosing the right people means first identifying those who not only have the technical vision, but also the business vision and the experience, discipline and tenacity to execute to that vision to achieve the results. It's that simple.

Leaders demonstrate the company values through actions. Leaders' ambition should be for the company and not for themselves. Steve Sanghi, CEO of Microchip, said it best in his book *Driving Excellence*: "The CEO ensures a consistency of purpose throughout the organization—goals, objectives, and values are well understood by all employees. The management structure is kept relatively flat, with the lowest feasible headcount maintained. The CEO regularly communicates to employees on the state of the company and the marketplace."[125] Leaders role-model the values as if they are convictions. They don't treat

---

[124] Employee name withheld for confidentiality.

[125] Steve Sanghi and Michael Jones, *Driving Excellence* (Hoboken, NJ, John Wiley & Sons, Inc., 2006), 29-30.

them as just appealing slogans that may or may not reflect how management really acts. Convictions hold true even when it's not convenient and through difficult periods.[126] Leadership at Intel is sorely lacking, and managers tend to nurture the "I" rather than the "we." It's plain to see why most employees don't trust and respect their managers. Hire and promote managers who have the talent to manage people and who practice the Values.

### 3.   *What happened to meritocracy?*

Results are what mattered in the Grove era. They *still* should matter. There needs to be more science behind grooming and assessing leaders. Measure what counts and pay for it. Years of service and grade level do not equal intelligence or the ability to execute. There are too many examples at Intel of people being promoted for no apparent reason related to business or results, and even more examples of people being promoted to vice president simply because they manage 500 people and have been with Intel for 20 years. That's not meritocracy—that's nepotism. Intel was once an engineering-driven culture, yet it has strayed away from scientific observation and measurement of business processes, as well as from the work people perform. It's time to measure results. The authors have seen many examples of middle and senior managers spinning metrics to make them look good when they have absolutely no effect on Intel's bottom line. Shame on their managers for trusting their data! It's one thing for a manager to set expectations; it's another to inspect the results to determine if the behaviors and results are real, can be measured, and tied back to the company's goals and objectives. If everyone's work isn't tied to the company's top or bottom line, then why are they doing it?

Employees will remain with a company because they like their jobs, managers, the culture, career opportunities, or other tangible and intangible things. Where there is a concerted effort to hire, train, and promote from within to advance both the culture and the career growth of employees, there is also a need to know whom to keep, and whom to let go when people do not meet the performance and cultural expectations. An example from a recent employee indicates where some of Intel's practices stand with respect to continuous improvement. An employee

---

[126] Ibid

was managing the operations for a product group, with about 20 direct reports. He did an exceptional job that warranted a promotion. His manager denied the promotion, so the employee left the group and took a job in another organization. The manager then hired two people in his place and gave both of them the promotion to the grade level the first employee had been expecting. When he found out, he confronted the manager, who said that he'd had to do it because he didn't want the two people to leave him stranded without an operations manager. He hired two-in-the-box, just in case one left. This example is but one of many that exemplifies what's wrong with a culture that does not pursue excellence.

### 4.   Why aren't clear goals formulated and communicated?

Wanting to grow revenue to $70 billion a year by 2009 is a lofty goal; however, everyone wants to know the specifics. Is the revenue growth expectation linear or is it back-end loaded? What markets will Intel serve? Who are the customer segments? How many new product introductions will it take per quarter to hit the revenue goal? What is the revenue target for each product? What is the market share target for each customer segment? Are you looking for a one-product wonder like microprocessors or are you expecting to achieve this revenue goal by selling more products to the same customers? What is the new customer acquisition goal for emerging markets?

These are simple questions that, at a minimum, must be answered internally so that every employee understands what your leadership is attempting to do. Inspire commitment to a clear vision with specific, definite objectives. Performance should be measured against corporate goals. At the corporate level, operational performance is measured in revenue, costs, earnings, and so forth. The focus should be on aligning specific business processes to those goals and then measuring the results. Functional groups and individual performance should be aligned to the performance of the processes and corporate goals. People need to understand how the work they do is tied to Intel's achievement of its goals and objectives. Outside of the factory, it is not obvious to people that what they are working on connects back to Intel's corporate strategy and objectives. Vision, mission, strategies, financial models, and business plans and objectives should be aligned throughout the organization and practiced in accordance to the company Values.

People are still acting as if all Intel needs to do is announce its products and the market will come running. It's time to remove the arrogance from the culture. Face it, those days are over. You got lucky with the microprocessor; the rest of your products will actually take some effort to sell.

**5.  *Why can't Intel compete when it's not the 800 lb. Gorilla?***

Intel's track record in non-microprocessor markets is atrocious. It's as if Intel can't compete unless it starts out in first place. What are the margin requirements? Who are the dominant players? What is our strategy to come from behind and win? What timeline does management want to set? How much will it cost to compete in these markets? How will we differentiate our products to gain market share? None of these questions were ever answered or understood across the employee base, and the acquisitions in the late 1990s never panned out. Intel has nothing to show for the $10 billion in acquisitions except financial losses. Senior management has to understand the basis of competition in markets where Intel is not dominant. What does it take to compete in non-core markets? Besides a good product, what are the other requirements? Clearly, time-to-market, supply chain agility and cost were critical in networking and communications markets; why weren't these areas addressed?

**6.  *Does Intel know what it means to be customer centric?***

During the PC boom years, Intel's market dominance afforded the company the luxury of having as its customers anyone who could afford a PC. There were few choices for consumers, and even fewer competitors. With the advent of the Internet and the explosion of personal electronic devices, people and companies no longer need a PC for connectivity: they can connect to the Internet now with cell phones and personal digital assistants (PDAs), and soon they'll connect with set-top boxes, game consoles, etc. Enjoying a monopoly position, Intel has never really had to focus on the customer. History has shown in telecommunications (think AT&T) that innovation is absent when one company has sole control over a technology or market. Microsoft is the latest example. There is a critical inflection point that Intel must confront, and it involves truly understanding customer needs and addressing those needs with platforms that customers choose over other alternatives. Intel must stop building products and throwing them into the market, thinking that people will buy them because they have Intel inside. Intel must reflect on past behaviors that have alienated customers and suppliers, and turn over a new leaf in its history book. Customers now have choices, and many of them are not choosing Intel. Intel must face this reality and answer the question, "Why are customers not choosing Intel?" There are lessons that can be learned if managers get in touch with the customer experience. How many senior managers meet with customers on a regular basis? More importantly, how many of those senior managers take actions to make the customer experience better? The answer is obvious—none. It is extremely difficult to conduct business with Intel. This needs to change very quickly: somebody's career should be on the line for improving the customer experience. The Customer Excellence Program and its predecessor have not improved customer satisfaction for the last 10 years. It's time to sit down with customers, understand their objectives and satisfaction requirements, and put in place the necessary actions and metrics to make it a reality. Remove the trappings of status and hierarchy that concentrate senior management's attention on internal metrics: make their focus and their pay directly tied to pleasing customers.

### 7.   What happened to Intel's Continuous Improvement Culture?

Continuous improvement cultures are built on employee empowerment, problem solving, merit, and the results-oriented pursuit of pleasing customers. All human resources and organizational systems should be structured to reward these behaviors and infuse them into the DNA of the culture. In the current Intel culture, there is avoidance of hard work above a certain grade level. In a culture of continuous improvement, grade levels would dictate the difficulty and scope of problem solving—not entitlement. Continuous improvement also implies taking a holistic approach for enterprise optimization, not a functional or sub-optimization approach. Sooner or later, the high margins experienced in fab manufacturing will no longer be sufficient to cover the deficiencies in supply chain management or time-to-market for new product introductions.

Looking to the future, the platform strategy may actually be a good move, as it puts more emphasis on Intel's traditional strengths in microprocessors, but it lacks a true execution plan that everyone from every functional area can understand. And if such a plan were in place, many changes would be required in order to successfully execute to that plan. Bureaucracy must be obliterated and it must start at the top. There are far too many management layers between those who do the work and those with the fancy titles. The latest actions give the appearance of cleaning out the dead weight, however the reality is much different. Senior managers have not demonstrated the courage to remove those people whom they have known for 20 or more years, unless they are the people who have challenged the status quo or ventured out of their immediate network. Everyone must truly live the Intel Values by demonstrating them, role-modeling them, and being held accountable for them. Demonstrate with real actions that you serve Intel and not your own greed or loyalty to your sycophants. Hold everyone accountable to the same performance standards and show it. Public hangings might be good for a short while, to let the general employee population know that you are serious in taking action to do what is right for Intel. Show employees that they are valued, and they will respond with higher performance. You can't force it, it must come naturally. Remember one thing: having the right employees, fully engaged, is what makes Intel great, not the products or the branding. Without faith in the Intel Values, employees will not make the commitment in their hearts, no matter how many stock options you offer them.

# LOOKING AHEAD

# Chapter 10

# The Problem Now is Focus

The single biggest danger in business and life, other than outright failure, is to be successful without being resolutely clear about why you are successful in the first place.[127]

Robert Burgelman

Complexity is the enemy of focus.

Anonymous

A goal without a measure is just a wish.

Japanese Proverb

## Intel's Exquisite Focus

In the early days of Intel, long before the emergence of its exquisite focus on driving the microprocessor business, the company's core competence comprised process technology innovation and silicon design.

It was very clear from Andy Grove's research that the crown jewels of Intel manufacturing were tied to Moore's Law. This relationship between manufacturing and Moore's Law has proven itself during the boom years of the PC industry where the silicon requirements were simple, with low-mix high-volume products that could be pumped through the Intel fab behemoth.

No one can truly appreciate the number of patents that have gone into Intel's fab process technology development. Nor can anyone fully appreciate the amount of money invested in capital equipment development. If you've ever been in an Intel fab, you begin to realize where all the company's money has gone. The Intel fab network is one of

---

[127] Jim Collins, *Good to Great* (New York, NY, HarperCollins, 2001), 213.

the most high-tech, sophisticated, silicon-producing machines in the world. It hums like a well-tuned Ferrari. When the Intel fab machine is at peak capacity, it supplies the world with microprocessors. This is an amazing feat, considering that the process technology at 90 nanometers is approaching in scale to DNA inside the human cell. It is also a remarkable accomplishment for a company that is only 38 years old. The graphic below illustrates the structure Intel's competitive advantage during the PC boom years.

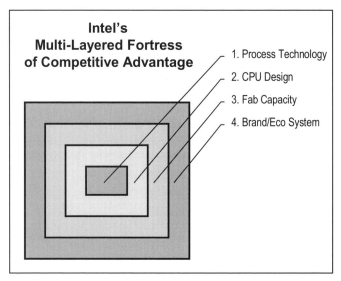

By the time Intel made the shift from memory to microprocessors, fab process technology was clearly in the driver's seat, with chip design taking a back seat. Intel would invest billions in process technology development to drive Moore's Law. At that critical inflection point, when Intel moved into microprocessors, the company was well positioned to be the sole supplier in the microprocessor market and to catch and ride the wave of the PC boom. Most of Intel's profits were invested into building more technologically advanced fabs to keep up with and chase demand. As the primary supplier in the marketplace for microprocessors, Intel had to build enough capacity not only to support the tremendous growth in demand, but also to maintain its virtual monopoly status. Even though Intel's senior management proclaims the worldwide fab capacity to be a competitive advantage, in reality, it has served as a virtual monopoly and a barrier to competition. No matter that AMD's products reign superior in the marketplace: AMD may never be able to catch up to Intel in terms of volume. The question is, does AMD have to catch up, or merely build enough capacity to profitably grow and take more market share away from Intel? In light of AMD's licensing arrangement with Chartered Semiconductor and its announcements to invest in new fabs in New York and Dresden, Germany, AMD seems poised to steal more market share, while Intel scrambles to get manufacturing in line with its revised product roadmaps.

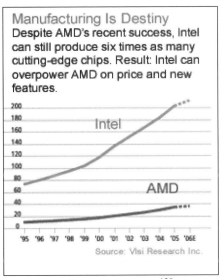

Source: VLSI Research[128]

By continuing to invest in fab process technology, Intel can produce six times as many chips as AMD, which gives Intel a short-term advantage in cutting prices on newer chips with more features. However, in the long term, this might not be the best strategy. In order to sustain revenue growth, recover its investments in fab technology and capacity, and maintain healthy margins, Intel must continue to sell more units. With the average selling price of microprocessors declining well below what was salable in the 1990s, Intel must now target emerging markets in China, Russia, South America, and Africa to sustain the volume growth needed to support fab investments. Computers are now selling for just under $300, because many of the people in these economies still can't afford a computer. Intel has resorted to subsidizing and sometimes even

---

[128] "Only the Paranoid Resurge" 2006,
http://www.forbes.com/free_forbes/2006/0410/042.html?partner=yahoomag

building computer "cafés" and "clubs" in these countries, in order to sell more of its products.

Ironically, Intel is becoming a slave to increases in process technology capabilities: its lack of true design innovation and silicon component integration have forced it to go to 65 nanometer (65 nm) process technology, just to stay ahead on volume and pricing. Remaining one generation ahead in process technology allows Intel to stay competitive with AMD's products, which possess superior designs. In this respect, Intel is clearly playing from behind. Probably the saving grace of the Barrett leadership was continuing Intel's lead in process technology, because clearly the attempts at diversification didn't pan out. Or possibly this was a strategic blunder on Barrett's part, because he didn't take into consideration the high overhead costs of the microprocessor model for supporting entry into those newer acquisition markets. He might have spent more time understanding the market dynamics of those acquisitions and invested in truly becoming a force to be reckoned with, rather than diverting company resources away from those markets.

Intel needed a market where it could sell 70-100 million units per year pumped through its global fab network, in order to generate those healthy margins which could fuel the growth in earnings and hence, stock price, that investors were accustomed to. In the midst of the Internet boom, Intel also needed to move quickly if it was going to capture some of the growth in communications and networking markets. The big question was, could Intel innovate quickly enough to bring new products to market and grow organically, or would the company attempt to grow through acquisitions? This was the monumental question facing Craig Barrett when he took over as CEO in 1998. We now know that instead of opting for organic or internal growth, the company went on a buying binge, gobbling up $10 billion worth of acquisitions. When you examine Barrett's strategic actions during the late-1990s acquisitions, it seems apparent that he never acquired a *precise* understanding of the specific capabilities that formed the basis of Intel's historical microprocessor-based core competency. Instead, when articulating "Intel's Core Strengths," he spoke in terms of generalities that *sounded* accurate but lacked the deep understanding and clarity required to set a course that would result in a significant competitive advantage.

Much internal speculation surrounds what the integration strategy was for those late-1990s acquisitions. If, at the time of the acquisitions, one thought of Intel in terms of its published strengths, there seemed to be a natural fit between the world's leading semiconductor manufacturer and the many acquired companies that were designing new silicon products but lacked manufacturing resources. Indeed, the intention of product marketing was to intercept the second-generation silicon from the acquisitions and move production into Intel factories. Surprisingly, the silicon from these acquisitions never made it into Intel's fab network, revealing that these products were unable to leverage Intel's strengths because the advantage of those strengths pertained primarily to microprocessors. It appears that neither Andy Grove nor Craig Barrett understood what the gaps were for moving from a CPU-centric, low-mix high-volume manufacturing environment to any of the other variations, especially those seen in telecommunications and networking, where the product mix tends to be high-mix low-volume.

Arguably, Barrett took a shotgun approach to the $10 billion in investments made during the first two years of his tenure as CEO. It is not apparent that he fully understood the narrowness of Intel's niche in microprocessors. Without fully comprehending what it would take to internalize manufacturing for these acquisitions, it seems he assumed that what had worked for Andy Grove in microprocessors would work for him in other markets. So with reckless abandon, Intel bought up any company perceived as a leader in communications and networking silicon that Intel could tie back into its core microprocessor business. The fact that Intel outsources silicon manufacturing to this day attests to the lack of planning for manufacturing integration prior to these acquisitions. When it came to actually producing the communications and networking silicon of its acquisitions, it seems that Intel lacked the passion for manufacturing these products in-house, lacked best-in-class capabilities (low cost, high performance advantages) geared for these products, not just microprocessors, and lacked a compelling value proposition for its customers, which would bring in high-margin sales.

It also appears that Intel was either blind concerning the time-to-market requirements for networking and communications products or assumed they were similar to the eighteen-month microprocessor time-to-market requirements. The basis of competition in these new markets was quite different from that of the CPU market, and significant changes would be needed if they were to become number one or number two. Time-to-market was absolutely critical, as was supply chain agility, but neither had been critical for success in the microprocessor market where Intel was the dominant player. Only after the acquisitions were made did it become apparent that Intel would struggle mightily to meet the time-to-market requirements for the acquisitions, which were about one-third those of the microprocessor market. Intel insiders were finding out the hard way that if they couldn't get a product out the door within six months, they would have to kill the product and miss the revenue opportunity.

Typical of a plan born of overconfidence, Intel's strategy for these new markets simply mirrored its "if we build it, they will buy it" microprocessor strategy. Employees from the acquisitions quickly tired of the cumbersome Intel practices being forced upon them when the market wanted expediency. Barrett paid much lip service to Intel's strength in silicon and how that would translate into success in these markets, when the reality was in fact grim. We now know that the acquisition strategy was a major failure. By and large, the Intel Communications and Networking groups lost money throughout Barrett's tenure as CEO and have continued to lose ever since. Looking back, it appears that the acquisition strategy was not based on a deep understanding of the realities (manufacturing and marketing requirements) for the acquisitions to be successful and win market share in the new markets.

Moreover, it appears that the acquisition foray may also have distracted Intel from retaining one of its competitive advantages, namely its strength in microprocessor design. In 1999, while Intel was enamored and consumed with its growth-through-acquisition strategy, AMD was quietly laying the foundation for its "Hammer" microprocessor architecture, a move that would arguably catapult the scrappy underdog into the position of microprocessor design leader by 2003. Of course, it's difficult to stay on top forever, but given the enormous differences between the two companies' research and development budgets, it appears that the focus on acquisitions may have distracted Intel enough to "open the door" for AMD to take the lead in microprocessor design, dangerously decreasing the strength of Intel's competitive advantage.

Clearly, there were lapses in focus with those acquisitions. The huge investments in process technology are not sustainable in the lower-margin non-microprocessor markets unless they can be supported with huge product volumes similar to those in microprocessors. Paul Otellini appears to have understood that the acquisitions were a diversion, and by changing to a Platform strategy, he took the money-losing businesses and paired them with the different segments of microprocessor products. This latest strategy is suspect because it still has the microprocessor cash cow subsidizing the money-losing, lower-margin businesses. The authors believe that this encourages a lazy culture among non-microprocessor personnel, because senior management know they will not be individually held accountable for failure to generate profits in those non-microprocessor businesses, as long as they use those businesses to augment the microprocessor sales. We think that this is a "Wal-Mart strategy," whereby the chipsets are the loss leaders to sell more microprocessors. It's sad to think that Intel management believes that this is a viable, long-term growth strategy. The platform strategy is still a microprocessor strategy that lacks true product innovation, and in the humble opinion of the authors, still does not have sustainable growth prospects.

## Multicore and the Loss of Intel's Design Leadership

Intel is not trying to achieve growth through product innovation: they're trying to preserve margins on existing microprocessor products by selling more of them re-branded as platforms (such as Viiv™).

Multi-core processors hold the promise of increased performance and greater efficiency than single-core chips. Some would argue that Intel's initial thrust into multi-core products with its dual-core microprocessors is merely a marketing-driven *reaction* to AMD's and IBM's leadership with multi-core products. One interesting post on an Internet message board discussed the release of Intel's first dual-core product and provided some keen insight into the company's culture of "results at all costs," gaming, and the apparent lack of managerial discernment or detail orientation:

> **Intel Engineers Now Trained Seals** – That's what their Marketing Management has turned them into, against their better judgment. Whenever confronted with a feature request, a good engineer would want to implement that feature in a manner that is both efficient and powerful. However with the "feature-check-box management" that is

currently in charge, the Intel engineers are now trained to find the easiest way to "check the box" [results at all costs]. Hence we have "dual core" chips that are in actuality "glue core." Meanwhile the Intel engineers are now getting plenty of sleep—a fringe benefit of having a manager that could not identify or understand a kludge if it bit him in the ass [lack of detail orientation]. The downside is that deep down the Intel engineers know they have sold their soul [gaming the system]. Look for some serious brain drain down the road…and yes, you could argue it has been happening for a while now.[129]

Was Intel's first dual-core product truly a "glue core" kludge, hastily put in place in order to give the aura of technical leadership and confuse the market at a time when AMD was releasing more elegant dual-core products? The benchmarking data would seem to indicate that this was the case. On May 9, 2005, *Tom's Hardware* published the results of their comparison tests between Intel's Pentium D and AMD's Athlon 64 X2 desktop dual-core microprocessors. Their conclusion stated, "Here's the bottom line. If we had to recommend a single core processor, the choice would depend greatly on the type of applications in use. But in the dual core arena, though, there is not much that speaks for Intel: go with the Athlon 64 X2."[130]

As of this writing, both manufacturers are producing dual-core products in volume, but how long before end-users stop differentiating between Intel and AMD for multi-core microprocessors or microprocessors in general? In the April 7, 2005 issue of the *Wall Street Journal*, the technology pundit Walter Mossberg published his annual PC buyers' recommendations. Under the microprocessor section, here's what he had to say: "Processor speed is overrated. On Windows machines, any Intel Celeron or Pentium microprocessor chip, or any AMD microprocessor, regardless of speed, will do fine at the most common computing tasks." One year later, Mossberg's column still carries the same message: "For stripped down Vista, a processor running at 800 megahertz or faster should be sufficient."[131] Should Mr. Mossberg's views be reflected in consumer buying patterns, then Intel's move to platforms could be another speed-bump in an already commoditized PC market. Time will tell.

Of late, in the server market segment, Intel has not been so fortunate.

---

[129] finance.messages.yahoo.com, message 1171840, April 12, 2005.
[130] www.tomshardware.com/cpu/20050509/dual_core_athlon-20.html
[131] *Wall Street Journal*, Annual PC Buying Guide, April 13, 2006.

Customers continue to look for the highest-performing, lowest-power-consuming microprocessors. Tom Yager, chief technologist of *InfoWorld's* test center, wrote of Intel in March 2006:

> The company's present take on lower power is backed with some specious marketing that pretends the CPU is the only system component that draws current. AMD's Opteron core has its own level 2 cache, in an approach that differs from Intel's shared cache. But Intel's vaunted shared core advantages are offset by Opteron's Direct Connect architecture that runs dedicated HyperTransport bus links among all cores in a multi-processors, multi-core server, not just across cores within a single physical CPU. Opteron also incorporates on-chip memory and I/O controllers, the architectural features that leave Intel in the dust on performance no matter how fast Intel cranks its front-side bus and memory hub. Opteron has neither an FSB nor a memory hub. These are not only factors in performance but also in total system power consumption—the basis of an honest performance-per-watt analysis—because Opteron systems are simpler in design and require fewer components than Intel's.[132]

Intel is at greatest risk in its extremely high-margin server business, where AMD has already captured over 20% of the market segment share and will inevitably grow, given Dell's latest decision to use Opteron for certain multi-processor (four- and two-way) servers with further plans to introduce AMD processor-based Dimension desktops and laptops. Unlike Intel, which was always arrogant regarding its products, Dell finally listened to customers after realizing the hard way (announcing that first quarter earnings in 2006 had fallen short of expectations) that the losses in their most profitable segment, the high-end multiprocessor servers to corporate customers, were more costly than reneging on their loyalty to Intel. It is the authors' belief that the economics of the Dell-Intel model are no longer conducive to profitable growth. Intel's price-performance model brought low-cost economics to the high-end server market, essentially killing a profitable category for companies like Sun Microsystems. Then Sun adopted AMD's Opteron, as did Hewlett-Packard and IBM, effectively circling Dell's wagon while delighting corporate customers. There's no longer any value-add in commodity systems or components touting price-performance. The new economic model is total cost of ownership, and AMD has demonstrated that Opteron offers value-add in the eyes of the customer, thereby changing

---

[132] Tom Yager, "Processor Race Revs Up," *InfoWorld.com.*, March 27, 2006, page 24.

the nature of the supplier-OEM relationship. The Dell announcement is a damaging blow to Intel's reputation for performance leadership and, more importantly, will most likely be very damaging to its bottom line.

Intel, of course, is pronouncing that its product roadmap will put it back into the performance lead across all microprocessor product segments in late 2006 or early 2007, but that remains to be seen because AMD will not be standing still while Intel tries to catch up. For now, it's clear that Intel no longer possesses unquestionable leadership in microprocessor design, which represents a weakening in one of the pillars of its competitive advantage.

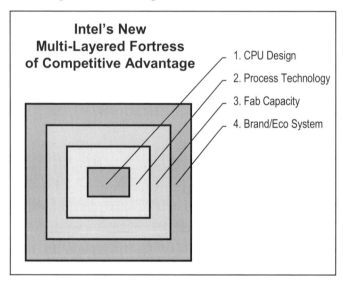

The bottom line, in our view, is that Intel should make product design its main focus and make fab process technology development subservient to it. This would be a huge shift in culture for the company—much like IBM's switch to a focus on services instead of mainframe computers. In recent years, Intel has used process technology superiority to make up for poor product designs. But AMD is now kicking Intel's butt, because customer need is driving design, and design is leveraging process technology. You don't see AMD moving to 65 nanometer process technology as quickly as Intel. They are able to sell their microprocessors at a premium to Intel's: where Intel's factory roadmap drives the microprocessor roadmap, at AMD, it's the other way around—and that's why they've taken the lead.

It's also interesting that AMD decided to spin off its flash business as it was losing too much money, especially since Intel would use its microprocessor profits as a buffer to instigate price wars in the flash market. AMD couldn't afford to lose money on microprocessors just to stay competitive in flash, so it pulled a bold move by spinning off the flash business, deciding that it had to be a competitive, profitable business on its own. For the past several years, AMD has had to use profits from its memory business to survive a brutal CPU market. It has learned to be profitable in a non-CPU area where there is a level playing field for the competition, and it did well in that area until Intel dramatically lowered flash memory prices in the fourth quarter of 2004 (which led to AMD's huge quarterly loss).

We believe that the lessons AMD learned in a more competitive non-CPU market have helped them become a leaner operation overall. Now that they have design leadership in CPUs, all they have to do is keep driving their designs, knowing that they have better, leaner operations overall than Intel, which must stay one generation ahead with process technology to compete. Intel could afford to lose money on flash as long as they were making money on microprocessors. Without the ability to use flash as a pricing diversion with AMD, Intel must decide whether it wants to use price wars in microprocessors to preserve (or gain) market share. Historically, price wars are not a winning strategy, especially in commodity markets. The competition between AMD and Intel is based on two different approaches, with the emphasis on different aspects of the technology. Intel is basing their research and development (R&D) emphasis on fab process technology, and executing that strategy in its vast fab network to maximize for high-volume output. This strategy requires a high-volume market to be profitable and feasible, especially if Intel wants growth beyond the core PC market. Should the market soften, then Intel will be left with excess inventory that they will have to burn off—possibly at a loss. AMD, on the other hand, is emphasizing "customer-centric" microprocessor chip design, and a gradual buildup of fab capacity. AMD is playing a perfect strategy for its size, designing better chips and aiming for the high end of the market, where volume is great, but if you don't have it, you can still make a profit on higher-margin products with lower fixed costs. In AMD's strategy, there are also advantages of lower depreciation costs, fewer employees, and less risk in a downturn. Since Paul Otellini isn't an engineer, he may not understand what the competition's CEO, Hector Ruiz, is doing, but it appears that Hector Ruiz has changed the rules of the game. AMD's recent acquisition of ATI's graphics chip business throws yet another curve ball at Intel. AMD hasn't yet revealed its plans, but has openly stated that it's considering open-sourcing a functional subset of ATI's graphic's drivers, which (as Tom Yager writes) "might affect a buying decision or two."[133] Furthermore, Yager points out that "an Intel motherboard with...an AMD chipset" could potentially become "a popular configuration" for PCs, and if this happens, it could be a "nightmare" for Paul Otellini.[134]

In view of this situation, other important questions come to mind: how much longer can Intel build factories and capacity before there is overcapacity? And how will that capacity help if the company isn't building products with the design features customers demand? The volumes just don't seem to be there to justify endless growth in capacity. Intel's capacity advantage already serves as a barrier to any new players entering the microprocessor market. Intel has begun to lose market share and they now have to face the reality that they can't keep losing money in all these other businesses just to maintain microprocessor leadership. Indeed, it begs the question of whether fab capacity should be demoted to number four on the "Multi-Layered Fortress of Competitive Advantage."

## The Next Frontier – The Battle for the Living Room

> Vision without action is a daydream. Action without vision is a nightmare.
>
> Japanese Proverb

Most investors think there is a battle raging for control of the digital home, pitting the cable companies, the phone companies, computer companies, Google, Apple, Yahoo, Microsoft, and the entire consumer electronics industry against one another in a fight to the death. Some even say that Apple has won this battle.[135] Even Cisco, with its acquisition of Scientific Atlanta, is aiming for the consumer indirectly by

---

[133] Tom Yager, "AMD Talks about ATI," Informationweek, August 8, 2006, page 16.
[134] Ibid.
[135] Fortune online, "Steve Jobs owns your living room," http://money.cnn.com/2006/01/27/technology/pluggedin_fortune/

owning the hardware that will deliver the content over cable networks. The battle for the living room no doubt promises to be one of the bloodiest global corporate battles of the next 10 years. The big news at the 2006 International Consumer Electronics Show (CES) was Intel's formal announcement of Viiv™, its latest platform for entertainment PCs. What should make this battle interesting is that it will pit consumer electronics incumbents like Sony, Panasonic, and Samsung against the likes of IBM, Apple, Intel, and Microsoft, to name a few.

## The Battle for the Living Room

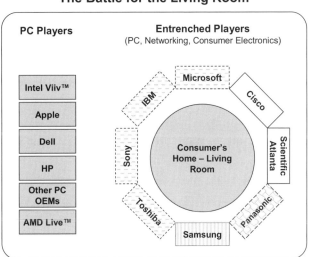

Although the cable and telephone companies are critical players in this battle, our discussion will focus only on the computer and consumer electronics companies. In the graphic above, we depict what we believe has already taken place with respect to marketplace positioning. The consumer electronics companies have been entrenched in the consumer's living room for some time, in one form or another (flat screen TVs, DVD players, VCRs, game consoles, etc.). Microsoft recovered from the poor showing of its first-generation game console to grab a significant stronghold in the living room. Cisco has entered the living room with its acquisition of Scientific Atlanta, and IBM through its alliance with Sony and Toshiba on the Cell processor. In essence, these companies have circled their wagons around the consumer's living room, in effect creating a proverbial barrier to PC manufacturers like Dell or HP and semiconductor players like Intel and AMD. Apple is clearly a wildcard, as demonstrated by its hurricane success with the iPod™.

### Intel and Apple

As mentioned previously, Intel has launched its new platform, Viiv™, for the next generation of entertainment PCs. Couple this with Apple's decision to go with Intel architecture for all its PC offerings, and you have the makings of an interesting partnership. It's interesting because Apple is probably the most innovative company to spring out of Silicon Valley. Not only did Apple enter the digital music player market with a late offering, it did so with the kind of extravaganza for which CEO Steve Jobs is renowned, and soon captured 80% of the market. Jobs also showed acumen with his decision to build the next-generation Apple operating system (OS) based on Unix, which freed it from most hardware constraints and gave Apple a competitive edge over Microsoft, because its OS is eminently more secure and reliable than Microsoft's (Windows). The question is what will Apple do for the living room now that it has a new architecture platform like Viiv™? Apple has begun by introducing its first product, the Intel-based Mac Mini for the living room. Starting at just $599, the Mac mini is the most affordable way to enjoy iLife '06, the next generation of Apple's award-winning suite of digital lifestyle applications, and features the Apple Remote and Front Row so you can play your music, enjoy your photo slideshows, watch your DVDs, iMovies, music videos, and television shows from across the room. "With the new Mac mini, Apple has now moved 50 percent of its entire product line to Intel within 60 days—a record transition," said Philip Schiller, Apple's senior vice president of Worldwide Product Marketing in the press release.[136]

It remains to be seen, though, whether the Mac mini will be a "TiVo killer." One should not discount any attempt by Steve Jobs to get into the living room—if he wants to enter the consumer's living room, he will. The iPod™ was successful because Steve Jobs created a holistic user experience, starting with the sleek design of the iPod™ and then the Nano,™ creating iTunes™ software that was usable on a PC or a Mac, and then finally, making music cheaply available as a download from the Apple website. If Apple decides to enter the consumer's living room,

---

[136] Apple introduces new Intel-based Mac mini, Feb. 28, 2006, http://macdailynews.com/index.php/weblog/comments/8730/

more than likely it will repeat the business model that made the iPod™ successful, and the Mac Mini might just be a transitional product until Apple's true offering, a new gadget called iTV becomes available. iTV, which is projected to go on sale in spring of 2007 for $299, will be marketed as "the missing link" between the Mac and the TV, allowing movies downloaded from iTunes to be streamed wirelessly from the PC or Mac to the big screen TV in the living room.[137] Intel, unfortunately, did not thoroughly think through the ecosystem for Viiv™ to be truly revolutionary in the living room. It is a weak entry in an already tired PC market. So, many questions are still left unanswered. How many PC users will convert to Apple? Better yet, how many will make the leap to manage two different platforms in the same home? Even with Apple's new software to run OS X and Windows, who wants the hassle?

### Cisco, Linksys and Scientific Atlanta

Cisco has said that video and IPTV (Internet Protocol television) are an integral part of its strategy for entering the home market. The company's acquisition of KiSS Technology, which makes DVD recorders and players that can be networked, along with its acquisitions of Linksys (a home networking manufacturer) and Scientific Atlanta (a maker of home networking and television set-top boxes) puts Cisco into a formidable position to offer the kind of products and services that will be in demand from home consumers. Although Cisco has stated that it intends to partner with existing players like Apple, one cannot ignore that in some areas, it will be competing with the likes of Sony and Samsung. Cisco has yet to prove itself outside of its core router business, but it has made respectable inroads in the VoIP (voice over Internet Protocol) markets, ahead of the former Bell companies. Cisco is loaded with cash and will more than likely execute its living room strategy, provided that it makes its products easy to use. Another interesting competitive tidbit is that Broadcom is providing the broadband chip for processing and recording video on Scientific Atlanta's latest Personal Video Recorder set-top box. All Cisco needs to do is complete the PVR set-top box with wireless capability, and it will become a force to be reckoned with in the

---

[137] "Apple unveils its latest arsenal," September 26, 2006, http://money.cnn.com/2006/09/26/technology/movie_downloads.fortune/?postversion=20 06092613

living room. The set-top box market has been a tough market to crack for Intel, and there is no evidence that the new Viiv™ chip will be considered in future generations.

### The New Triumvirate: IBM, Toshiba and Sony

IBM has been in the semiconductor business for quite some time and was formerly a supplier of the Power PC chip to Apple. IBM entered into an arrangement with Sony and Toshiba to develop the next-generation Cell chip for broadband communications, and it's now targeting consumer electronics multimedia applications. The Cell processor's inside is vastly different from that of conventional processors. This tiny chip contains a powerful 64-bit, dual-threaded IBM PowerPC core, but also eight proprietary "Synergistic Processing Elements" (SPEs), essentially eight more highly specialized mini-computers on the same die. It's these SPEs that make the Cell architecture special, as you might guess: IBM describes the product as a "system-on-a-chip." And as with IBM's Power5 processors, multi-processing is build right into the die.[138] One of the most interesting properties of this new processor is its modular design. In addition to being essentially a multi-processor solution on a chip, each Cell processor can theoretically share its processing tasks with any other Cell processor anywhere, not just ones hooked up to the same system.[139] Overall, the IBM/Sony/Toshiba Cell processor has a bright future ahead of it, and not just because millions will be sold in PlayStation 3 consoles. With the correct compiling tools, Cell-inside PCs could potentially excel at the kind of applications consumers buy high-end PCs for today: graphics, video, audio, and games. Will they, though, in the face of Intel's upcoming Extended Memory-64 Technology and dual-core Pentium 4 processors?[140]

Both Sony, with its PlayStation, and Microsoft, with its XBox™, have decided to use the Cell chip for their systems. There has been quite a stir about using PlayStation and Xboxes for more than just gaming, and clearly, the chip has the capability to support digital multimedia applications. The power of the Cell chip is that it was specifically designed with the living room in mind. According to Howard Stringer,

---

[138] IBM's CELL Processor: Preview to Greatness?
http://www.pcstats.com/articleview.cfm?articleID=1727
[139] Ibid.
[140] Ibid.

Sony's CEO, the PlayStation 3 is designed to be at the center of the living room and will spearhead Sony's new digital strategy.[141] Cell's capabilities will allow it to deliver one trillion or more floating-point calculations per second (or "teraflop," a measure of a computer's speed). By way of comparison, it will have the ability to do 'north' of one trillion mathematical calculations per second, roughly 100 times more than a single Pentium 4 chip running at 2.5GHz. Cell will likely use between four and 16 general-purpose processor cores per chip. Peter Glaskowsky, editor in chief of *Microprocessor Report,* has pointed out that "A game console might use a chip with 16 cores, while a less-complicated device like a television set-top box would have a processor with fewer."[142] According to a ZDNet report,

> While Cell's hardware design might be difficult, it's creating software for the chip that will be the trickiest part of establishing it in the market. "It's going to take an enormous amount of software development," Doherty said. "We believe the chip architecture is going to be on time and ahead of the software wizardry that is going to really make it get up and dance." Furthermore, he said, creating an operating system and set of applications that can take advantage of the Cell's multiprocessing and peer-to-peer computing capabilities will be the key to determining if Cell will be successful. Knowing this, the three chip partners have so far set a goal of crafting Cell as an operating system with application software alongside the Cell hardware. Cell's designers are also engineering the chip to work with a wide range of operating systems, including Linux,[143] and the triumvirate's developers will use to test the chip's various features, such as its multimedia processing capabilities. They are also likely to form the basis of a Cell software development kit and the Cell OS and applications for end-devices, such as game systems. [144]

The collaboration of this triumvirate on the Cell processor naturally leads one to wonder what Microsoft has in store beyond the Xbox. Microsoft could, in effect, create an entirely new market by writing software for the Cell processor beyond just the Xbox for gaming. Imagine a completely new software architecture for the digital home, running on the Cell processor. This could become a strategic inflection

---

[141] *Wall Street Journal*, June 6, 2006, B1.
[142] John Spooner, "Chip trio allows glimpse into 'Cell,'" http://news.zdnet.com/2100-9584_22-948493.html
[143] Ibid.
[144] Ibid.

point on a scale of such magnitude that it could seriously damage Intel's existing business model. Intel could be left with Microsoft's entertainment PC edition, while Sony and Toshiba create consumer electronics that everyone "must have" in their living rooms, all based on this new software architecture from Microsoft—a leaner, meaner, more secure, feature-rich operating system that is extremely easy to use and optimized for the Cell processor. Of course, the latter scenario may be wishful thinking; it might be completely out of character for Microsoft to go down this path. But if you think about it, there are over 70 million baby boomers who will soon be retiring, looking to spend their money on the latest and greatest gadgets for the living room so they can watch movies on demand, play games with their grandchildren, show photos of their family, beam things to the cell phones and PDAs, and so on. It's unlikely that baby boomers will sit in their living rooms using Microsoft Office applications. The Cell processor offers much more than merely console-based gaming. While it may be wishful thinking to imagine Microsoft writing software specifically for Cell, one would at least expect them to optimize Vista to run on the Cell processor.

What does all this mean to Intel? Very simply, it means Intel must face some deeply entrenched competitors as it attempts to enter a new market (the living room), and it also means that it could potentially face more competition in its core markets. History has shown that Intel has not been successful in strategy formulation, as evidenced by its failed foray into networking and communications. According to Robert Burgelman, Intel's success in past strategy making "relied more on strategic recognition than on foresight. Intel had been lucky to invent the microprocessor and even luckier to obtain the design win for the IBM PC."[145] Intel parlayed that luck to develop and enjoy one of the more remarkable competitive advantages found in the history of business, and its disciplined focus on a microprocessor-based core competency has created unimaginable wealth for the company and thousands of investors. Surprisingly, as manifest by the failure of Intel's acquisition strategy, the competency has proven to be narrower than one would think. Moreover, evidence suggests that senior leaders at Intel possess more hubris than precise understanding regarding company strengths, advantages, and

---

[145] Robert A. Burgelman, "Strategy as Vector and the Inertia of Coevolutionary Lock-in," *Administrative Science Quarterly* 47 (2002): 331.

obvious weaknesses—especially Intel's physical and cultural fragmentation (which, historically, has been masked by Intel's profitability). Furthermore, looking at history, it appears that Intel has not yet put the right people into the right positions to successfully attack and overcome this fragmentation monster. Yet it is important to do so, because in the 21$^{st}$ century world of the digital home, execution will be king. If the IBM/Toshiba/Sony triumvirate can execute, it will be formidable competition for Intel; thus Intel will be attacked by AMD on the front and IBM/Toshiba/Sony on the flank. The other challenges will be trying to manage a new customer like Apple, while keeping existing customers like Dell from giving more of their microprocessor business to AMD, and dealing with a partner like Microsoft on Vista, while managing Microsoft as competitor (Xbox with Cell chip). This is all uncharted territory for a company that doesn't have a respectable track record for devising strategies to be competitive where it's not the dominant player, and Intel doesn't have a respectable track record or reputation for being easy to do business with—a disadvantage when trying to enter new markets. Late 2006 and early 2007 will be the defining era for Intel. The company no longer can claim the title of undisputed technology leader when speaking of its products, and the same may eventually be true of its manufacturing processes as well.

## Outsourcing Innovation

The Viiv™ platform appears to be a good strategic maneuver because it leverages the microprocessor model in a new (home electronics) market. The goal of this platform is to stimulate home owners to purchase another electronic box for their living room. The problem is that Intel is branding it as a PC for the living room and will attempt to sell it for a relatively high average selling price. The problem with this strategy is that the "sweet spot" price point for most electronics in the living room, even on the high end, is around $300-$400, and even that price point doesn't last long, as demonstrated by DVD players and DVD recorders. Prices eventually come down as volumes go up. It makes one question whether people are going to buy it in the volumes Intel is expecting.

Intel has hyped the latest design win with Apple as a huge opportunity. One must question why this represents such a huge opportunity when

Apple only has about 2% PC market share worldwide. Even if Apple's share doubles in the next two years, it still won't make much of a dent in Intel's revenue growth. The authors believe that the primary reason for Intel's desire to acquire Apple's business is, in effect, to "outsource" innovation and rely on Apple to innovate new products that carry Intel's silicon. Apple's iPod wasn't a niche player in the portable music/mp3 market—it had volumes that clearly attracted Intel. One thing for sure is that Apple is still able to command higher prices for its PCs, but the advent of its new software that enables Apple PCs to run Windows leaves us wondering whether it will benefit Apple. In fact, we noticed postings online that ran the gamut from "the best hardware can now run the worst operating system," to "by going to the Intel architecture, Jobs finally gets the economies of scale that all Wintel manufacturers enjoy. And by making his machine supportably a dual-boot machine, corporate IT decision makers have no barrier to choosing Mac."[146] After all, Apple always wanted to be "different," yet it's now giving in to the "enemy" by allowing the competitor's software to run on Apple machines. Moreover, if Apple is doing all the innovating to come up with new premium products, how willing will it be to share profits with a component supplier such as Intel, and still be competitive? "Apple, beware of commoditization!" The world awaits Apple's next move, and Intel is certainly waiting in the wings to take advantage of this entry into the large consumer electronics market. On the surface, it does appear to be a good strategy for Intel, but it's still not clear how it will play out.

In a way, Intel had to do it because it has been funding research in the PC market for OEM's like Dell and HP, not to mention the others in Asia. The PC market has been commoditized for years and will only get worse. IBM's divestiture of its Thinkpad™ line to Lenovo in order to focus more on servers, software, and services, and Hewlett-Packard's similar moves, leave Dell with a dilemma over continued earnings growth. Dell's recent acquisition of Alienware demonstrates some parallels to the Intel/Apple relationship. Both are trying to get out of commodity businesses by acquiring premium product brands (Dell directly, Intel indirectly), hoping to charge more money to ignite profit growth. The problem is that neither of these strategies offers high

---

[146] XP on a Mac? Readers weigh in,
http://www.computerworld.com/softwaretopics/os/macos/story/0,10801,110256,00.html

volumes, but possibly may offer higher profit potential if the companies can address a niche market and grow it beyond its current size.

For Intel, these developments might not change the downward direction of its profit per unit. The latest strategic moves Intel has made are consistent with its "quick fix" gestalt culture. Try to grab some quick profits from the Apple venture, while trying to figure out what to do for long-term growth. Unfortunately, Intel can't show where growth will be coming from or how it can sustain earnings growth when it's still selling non-microprocessor products at a loss.

Paul Otellini's "platformization" of Intel may temporarily have the potential to shore up Intel's competitive position, as we've seen with the introduction of the Viiv™ platform. However, Intel's fragmentation monster will continue to rear its ugly head, as business process complexity increases with the introduction of more platforms, which will require more business process integration and scalability to enable exquisite execution that meets customer demands. Intel's strategy for addressing complexity has always been to add more headcount. Now that its previously unassailable advantage in microprocessor-based markets is being challenged on many fronts, its influence appears to be waning, and one wonders whether Intel has spread itself too thin. It's still not clear what the company's focus is, nor was it ever clear to us or our fellow employees. Now, as then, Intel seems like a rudderless ship, without a genuine captain on board.

# Chapter 11

# Rethinking the Culture

One man practicing sportsmanship is better than 50 men preaching it.[147]

Knute Rockne

Courage is what it takes to stand up and speak; courage is also what it takes to sit down and listen.[148]

Sir Winston Churchill

Business begins with trust...As companies abandon bureaucratic mechanisms, their leaders need to understand that trust is as important to management as it is to relationships with customers.[149]

Warren Bennis

The Intel culture has become a culture that can't help itself. It has deteriorated to the point where really talented people have left or plan to leave the company. There are many reasons why people want to leave and why people remain despite being disengaged. It's hard to say which is worse: people leaving or people mentally disengaging while staying with the company. The authors feel that the latter situation is more damaging, because it spreads like a cancer throughout a company. It eventually manifests itself as cultural helplessness, where everyone acknowledges that the culture has deteriorated but gives up trying to make a difference, having found that no one cares or that people get punished for speaking up. The authors have spoken to many employees

---

[147] Quote of the day, www.excite.com.
[148] Ibid.
[149] Ibid.

during our tenure at Intel, and unequivocally we have heard common themes, like "Hey, it's a paycheck," or "I just do what I'm told and go home and have a real life." The degree of dissatisfaction is truly disappointing, yet senior management does not acknowledge or seem to care how it has affected morale.

Intel has dual core (no pun intended) but conflicting purposes that have been in existence for quite some time. The first core purpose comes from the early days of Robert Noyce and Gordon Moore, who lived to create innovative technologies that changed the world. This was the founding core, the purpose of the company until the microprocessor was invented. The microprocessor did not really change the world until the invention of the personal computer. No one knew at the time how much the personal computer would change the world, but it was at that inflection point that Intel's second core purpose was born—pursuit of personal wealth. Many early employees were minted millionaires by the late 1980s or early 1990s. Many college graduates flocked to the high-tech world searching for wealth from stock options. This was the core purpose that took root in the Grove era, overwhelmed the culture during the Barrett era, and continues to be the primary motivator for many employee actions to this day. Ideally, corporate and employee wealth should come as a byproduct of effectiveness in driving a great company purpose, such as technology innovation. Instead, Intel's culture is being driven another way, in pursuit of personal gain. This duality of core purpose has created an unhealthy culture in which the Intel Values are trampled by those in the entitled class, or by those trying to get there.

This situation would seem in contrast to Craig Barrett's final communication to employees as CEO, when he stated that "the philosophy of Intel's two founders is still the heart and soul of Intel: Invest in R&D, be first in the market with new technology, believe the technology can change the world, and never look back. That is how the founders ran the company, and that is how we run the company today."[150] Taken at face value, Barrett's letter seems to reveal that throughout his career he was aligned with the initial core purpose of Intel as outlined by Robert Noyce and Gordon Moore, and his public comments reveal he believed that Intel, in general, was also so aligned.

After honoring Noyce and Moore, Barrett comments on his working

---

[150] Intel employee website, May 20, 2005

relationship with Andy Grove: "Over the years that I have worked with Andy, he always stressed the following: Be paranoid, be intellectually honest, be fair and firm in your dealings with employees and customers, don't be afraid to take risks, and, above all, always have a strategy to win. Andy's philosophy is reflected in our culture and is ingrained in our everyday actions." Despite Barrett's close association with Grove, the latter's emphasis on "winning" (making money, results at all costs) did not seem to corrupt Barrett's view of Intel's core purpose—to advance new technology. However, as we've seen, in his tenure as CEO, Barrett didn't have a strategy for winning with respect to the acquisitions, and it took him too long to replace people who publicly or internally failed, when he replaced them at all. Barrett was either disconnected from the reality of the Intel working environment or felt that he was above the task of *inspecting* the culture to make sure managers and employees were adhering to the Values. The authors believe it was the latter, based on his lip service and indifferent responses to the barrage of emails and open forum questions asking him to take action to eliminate bureaucracy and restore the health of Intel's culture.

With Paul Otellini, we get a different perspective. Shortly after becoming CEO, Otellini made some revealing comments at an open forum with Intel employees. During the question-and-answer portion of the meeting, one employee asked, "Why should we come to work? It used to be we all came to work for the [rising] stock price. Why do you [Otellini] come to work now?" His immediate, gut-level response was, "I want to retire with Intel being the company with the highest market cap [in the world]." Following this spontaneous response, he paused and then continued to talk about how he and the newly hired vice president of Marketing were putting significant effort into redefining the brand essence of Intel. He added, "No one is here because of stock options. We're here because we want to change the world."[151]

Was this second, more thoughtful answer really what Otellini was thinking? It would seem that his first response expressed what he really thought, and it was noticeable how he recoiled and then came up with a more politically correct answer—that of "changing the world"—which aligns with the initial core purpose of Intel. Indeed, is it too much of a stretch to surmise that his first thought betrayed his real thinking?

---

[151] Open Forum with Paul Otellini, June 10, 2005.

Perhaps not. Moreover, it speaks volumes about the entitled class and its core purpose of achieving personal gain.

Sadly, Intel's culture, comprised of IMBOs and mantras such as "results at all costs" and "you own your career," reinforces the gaming behaviors that typify the unspoken core purpose of personal gain, which drives Intel's culture of greed. Actions that protect the entitled class, who epitomize this core purpose, result in a culture that stifles progress. This explains why a company that is flush with cash was unable to succeed financially with its acquisition strategy during the Barrett era, when it attempted to penetrate new markets with new products. And in future years, we may be able to ascertain that this culture prevented success during the Otellini era, with its platforms strategy focusing on the penetration of new markets, largely with existing CPU products. Indeed, the pursuit of personal gain—especially in the absence of an enduring core purpose that has widespread employee understanding and buy-in— has resulted in an Intel with no soul beyond a rising stock price. The founders' vision of an egalitarian meritocracy, focused on innovation that changes the world, is dead.

As is shown in the table below, the Intel Values are clearly stated and, to the average person, would seem easy to incorporate into personal behavior and daily activities. As mentioned previously, the Values were written in 1986, 18 years after the founding of Intel, which would imply that a distinct culture, with distinct behaviors exhibited by the Intel leaders, had already taken root. A culture evolves through observation, practice, and imitation of behaviors, not so much by what is published as "values." The hardest part for any company, especially large and successful ones, is to align behaviors to published values. GE struggled with this for years, and it could be said that Jack Welch acquired his nickname "Neutron Jack" not solely because of all the layoffs, but because he had to fix poor operational performance by drumming up the courage to make difficult changes to GE culture in order to align behaviors to the published values. As we have shown, actual behaviors at Intel are deeply inconsistent with the Intel Values, and although we suspect that most of the employees in the entitled class would disagree with this claim, the majority of the expendable class would agree wholeheartedly with our observations.

| Intel Values | Actual Behaviors |
|---|---|
| **Risk Taking**<br>• Foster innovation and creative thinking<br>• Embrace change and challenge the status quo<br>• Listen to all ideas and viewpoints<br>• Learn from our successes and mistakes<br>• Encourage and reward informed risk taking | **Risk Aversion**<br>• Ingrained tendency to push back, resist change<br>• Punish those who challenge the status quo<br>• Many cases where lessons not learned from past mistakes<br>• There is a fear of retribution for risk taking |
| **Quality**<br>• Achieve the highest standards of excellence<br>• Do the right things right<br>• Continuously learn, develop and improve<br>• Take pride in our work | **Expediency**<br>• Less emphasis on doing the right things, more emphasis on doing things fast than right<br>• Little continuous improvement outside fab<br>• Rites of passage criteria into certain functional domains not clearly established |
| **Great Place To Work**<br>• Be open and direct<br>• Promote a challenging work environment that develops our diverse workforce<br>• Work as a team with respect and trust for each other<br>• Win and have fun<br>• Recognize and reward accomplishments<br>• Manage performance fairly and firmly<br>• Be an asset to our communities worldwide | **Great for Entitled Class**<br>• Focal punishment for being open and direct<br>• Performance managed unfairly, without rigor<br>• Focal a popularity contest and not a meritocracy<br>• Different accountability standards for entitled class and expendable class<br>• Perception of accomplishment is rewarded rather than actually measuring accomplishments, especially in senior management |
| **Discipline**<br>• Conduct business with uncompromising integrity and professionalism<br>• Ensure a safe, clean and injury-free workplace<br>• Make and meet commitments<br>• Properly plan, fund and staff projects<br>• Pay attention to detail | **Bureaucracy**<br>• Lack of attention to detail, especially among entitled class<br>• Over-staffed and poorly planned projects<br>• Lack of rigor and accountability for results and meeting commitments |
| **Results Orientation**<br>• Set challenging and competitive goals<br>• Focus on output<br>• Assume responsibility<br>• Constructively confront and solve problems<br>• Execute flawlessly | **Results At All Costs**<br>• Lack of accountability, especially when results not achieved<br>• Poor project execution, many schedule resets<br>• Reality not confronted or addressed<br>• Project resets are the norm |
| **Customer Orientation**<br>• Listen and respond to our customers, suppliers and stakeholders<br>• Clearly communicate mutual intentions and expectations<br>• Deliver innovative and competitive products and services<br>• Make it easy to work with us<br>• Be vendor of choice | **Inward Focus**<br>• Customer responsiveness lagging industry due to poor customer orientation<br>• Minimal Innovation outside of CPU<br>• Very difficult to work with Intel as both customer and supplier<br>• Customer satisfaction consistently below expectations and trending downward |

# EPILOGUE

# Reflections on the Culture

There will come a time when one must choose between doing the right thing and doing what's easy.

Professor Albus Dumbledore

Is the current crop of Intel senior managers capable of the sort of decisive action that is required to fix Intel's culture? History may already have passed judgment. While some analysts have suggested that the current and former CEOs (Otellini and Barrett) should be removed, the observations in this book and the latest thinking in evidence-based management suggest deeper changes are required in order to improve the long-term performance of Intel. An analogy would be that of a baseball team on a losing streak, whose manager gets fired. A new manager is brought in, but it's to lead the same bunch of players whose losing streak got the previous manager fired.[152] Intel's lackluster performance over the past eight years goes far beyond the actions of the Chairman and CEO; rather, it deeply permeates the management layers of the entitled class.

It's up to readers to draw their own conclusions about what should be done regarding Intel management's performance over the last eight years. Many talented individuals have already left the company for reasons more related to the sickness of the culture than the performance of the company stock. Recently, Paul Otellini announced a complete self-examination of the entire company to "restructure, re-size and repurpose"

---

[152] Jeffrey Pfeffer and Robert I. Sutton, *Hard Facts, Dangerous Half-Truths & Total Nonsense: Profiting from Evidence-Based Management* (Boston, MA: Harvard Business School Press, 2006), 192-193.

Intel for the future.[153] Larger questions will remain after the "restructuring" of Intel. Those questions will ultimately have to be dealt with by management. The problem of disconnection between the stated Values and the practice of those values is simple to diagnose, yet mammoth to fix. Wall Street has become impatient, and rightfully so, as Intel's existing management has had ample time since Andy Grove's departure as CEO to prove their management capability and worth to employees and shareholders. Paul Otellini might start off on the road to better financial health, but as we have tried to show, the road less traveled is the one that will restore the cultural health of a once-great, high-technology company.

---

[153]"Intel Announces Major Restructuring,"
http://www.mercurynews.com/mld/mercurynews/news/breaking_news/14445851.htm